The Calm Buddha at Bedtime

The Calm Buddha at Bedtime

Tales of Wisdom, Compassion and Mindfulness
to Read with Your Child

Dharmachari Nagaraja

WATKINS
Sharing Wisdom Since 1893

The Calm Buddha at Bedtime
Dharmachari Nagaraja

First published in the UK and USA in 2017 by
Watkins, an imprint of Watkins Media Limited
Unit 11, Shepperton House
89-93 Shepperton Road
London N1 3DF

enquiries@watkinspublishing.com

Development Editor: Kelly Thompson
Managing Editor: Fiona Robertson
Story Editor and Additional Writing: Lou Kuenzler
Copyeditor: Judy Barratt
Head of Design: Glen Wilkins
Production: Uzma Taj
Commissioned Artwork: Geraldine Rodriguez

A CIP record for this book is available from the British Library

ISBN: 978-1-78678-080-5

10 9 8 7 6

Typeset in Cantoria MT
Colour reproduction by XY Digital
Printed in China

www.watkinspublishing.com

Contents

About this Book

This is the third in the *Buddha at Bedtime* series of books, in which I retell traditional Buddhist stories with the aim of restoring compassion and mindfulness to children's often overstimulated and sometimes stressful lives. I hope that reading these stories before bedtime will help children let go of their anxieties and concerns at the end of each busy day and feel more ready for a deep, restorative sleep. Above all, through the stories I want to nurture an understanding that, despite being so young, children do in fact already have the tools, skills and "inner space" to deal with the many distractions, challenges and pressures that life might put in their path.

Through a wide range of settings, characters and predicaments, each story explores an aspect of the four primary Buddhist principles or values, known as the Four Noble Truths (see page 12), and of the Noble Eightfold Path (see pages 13–15), which the Buddha taught were fundamental to a contented life. At the end of every tale, a key lesson of the story is highlighted by Hotei, the Laughing Buddha (see opposite). I hope Hotei's words of wisdom, as well as the challenges and solutions encountered throughout each story, will encourage conversation between you and your child on all manner of topics. This way, you can explore your child's developing views about themselves and the world, and help them to process any difficulties they might be going through.

Choosing a story

You don't need to read the book from start to finish. Each night, encourage your child to choose a story based on the title that appeals most, or the picture or character they are drawn to. Alternatively, you could choose for them, based on key themes that you feel might help your child most at that particular time (the contents page gives a useful summary of these and there's an index of themes at the end of the book to help you, too). For example, if you are worried that your child is finding it difficult to be accepted into a new school or some other new situation, you might read "Tintoretto, the Mouse from Town"; or if you think your child is feeling sad about the loss of something or someone

Archie and Hotei

Two special characters will join you as you explore the pages of this book. The first is my wee dog Archie, who is hiding in each illustration, searching for the jewel of wisdom in each story, just as I hope you and your little listener will do, too. See if you can spot him! His patience, persistence and gleeful curiosity sum up a good approach to the Buddha's teachings. The second character is a little, rounded, happy chap called Hotei. Often referred to as the Laughing Buddha, he is not the Buddha himself, but the embodiment of an ancient Chinese Buddhist monk known for his generous nature and broad smile. You will see Hotei at the end of each story, where he offers some words of guidance and wisdom that encapsulate the story's central value.

(perhaps you've moved house, they've changed schools or they've suffered a bereavement), you might read "The Teddy Bear Tussle", with its theme of being brave and letting go.

Opening up to meditation

All the stories start by encouraging your child to relax and get ready to listen. This way of entering the world of storytelling helps to promote a less distracted, calmer, more receptive and more meditative state of mind (see pages 18–19 for more insight into the art of mindfulness). It also helps your child to navigate their way more easily over the horizon into sleep once the story is over.

At the end of the book you'll find three guided visualizations, as well as general suggestions for approaching meditation, which will allow you to gently introduce your child to a more structured meditation practice. A key aim is to increase awareness of how emotions reveal themselves in our physical body. These meditations will help to calm and centre your child and teach them to read their own body for signs of stress or anxiety, and react appropriately.

I hope that sharing this book with your child brings both of you enjoyment and contentment, as well as a little nourishing food for thought. As the famous Buddhist blessing goes:

May you be well, may you be happy, may you be free from suffering.

Who is the Buddha?

Born more than 2,500 years ago in what is now Nepal, the Buddha – at that time simply known as Siddhartha Gautama – wanted for nothing, living a life of luxury behind the walls of his family's many royal palaces. One day, he ventured out in search of new experiences and adventure, and was deeply shocked and disturbed by what he saw. On the dusty lanes of the city, people were suffering, enduring the pain of old age, sickness and death. These sights made him very unhappy and he retreated once again behind the palace walls.

However, his material wealth had lost its appeal, so eventually Siddhartha Gautama went out into the city again. This time he met a monk who was calm, happy and at peace. Young Siddhartha could not understand how the monk could be happy in a world that held so much misery, but, inspired, he decided he would leave his royal life to find true happiness. He travelled far and wide across India, training under many teachers and living a life of poverty and severe self-discipline that included periods of strict fasting. He also learned to meditate: to bring his mind into quiet focus in order to reflect, contemplate and find inner peace. Siddhartha persevered with his life of self-denial for six years but did not find the happiness he sought.

At a place called Bodhgaya, in northeastern India, Siddhartha sat down in the shelter of a bodhi tree. With steely determination, he vowed not to get up until he had discovered the secret of lasting happiness. He meditated deeper and deeper all through the night, until the meaning of life became clear to him and he experienced what we know of as his Enlightenment. Thereafter, he was known as the Buddha, meaning the "Awakened One".

After his Enlightenment, the Buddha was determined to share his understanding of the truth of life with as many people as would listen. He gave his first sermon to a group of monks who were angry that he had given up his life of denial, telling them about the Four Noble Truths (see page 12) that would lead to Enlightenment and true, lasting happiness. He travelled far and wide, using stories like the ones in this book to teach about the importance of living with compassion, generosity and wisdom. And he called his approach the Middle Way, indicating that these were a realistic set of values lying somewhere between austerity and indulgence. He encouraged his followers not simply to adopt his teachings, but to test them and experience them for themselves. In the same way, one of the most important lessons we can teach our children is that they have to find out for themselves what really makes them happy. We can guide, advise and comfort them, but in the end only they know their own true mind.

At the age of 80 years old, at Kushinagar in northern India, the Buddha lay down and died. His last words were, "Impermanence is inherent in all things. Work out your own freedom with diligence." It's said that as he died, the earth shook, blossoms fell from the sky as stars shot from the heavens, and the air was filled with celestial music.

What are the Buddha's Teachings?

The teachings of the Buddha, known as Buddhism, promote fundamental positive principles and practices that transcend time and culture. Today, approximately 350 million people worldwide follow the way of the Buddha. As well as providing guidance on ethical and moral behaviour, Buddhism offers practical strategies for how to cope with the anxieties and struggles of daily life, skills that can help both our children and us to flourish no matter what life throws at us.

The Three Jewels

In Buddhism, choosing the Buddha as a role model is known as "going for refuge to the Buddha". There are three established "refuges" in Buddhism – or things that help us along our journey – called the Three Jewels. Making them the guiding lights in your life means that you are following the path of Buddhism. The Three Jewels are:

* **The Buddha** – referring to the "ideal" of Buddhahood as well as to the historical Buddha himself;

* **The Dharma** – the collection of the Buddha's teachings and practices, which together provide a map that leads us to our goal;

✱ **The Sangha** – the people we travel with on our journey through life, and who help and encourage us to follow the way of Buddhism.

The Four Noble Truths

In addition, the Buddha identified the Four Noble Truths, Buddhism's founding principles. I have set these out below. Consider these in light of your own life and the lives of your children, who learn by your example:

✱ **First Truth:** Life inevitably involves suffering, whether physical or psychological. Many might find this view initially pessimistic. But for the Buddha this truth was neither optimistic nor pessimistic, simply realistic – the way things actually are.

✱ **Second Truth:** The reason we suffer is that we want things we do not or cannot have. Whether we want fame or fortune, or simply to be free from negative emotions (such as jealousy or anger), we become unhappy when life fails to live up to our expectations.

✱ **Third Truth:** The cure for suffering is to stop wanting. If we are prepared to make the effort to let go of our desire for what we don't have, happiness will follow. Of course many could argue that a better way to happiness would simply be to go and get the things we want. The Buddhist response is that we can never get everything we want, partly because the more we have, the more we want.

✱ **Fourth Truth:** The way to stop wanting more is to follow the Noble Eightfold Path, which focuses not on changing things around us, but instead on changing our own mind about how we view ourselves, things, others and life.

The Noble Eightfold Path

The Buddha taught that there are eight fundamental steps on the path to Enlightenment. He set these out clearly for his followers as:

* **Right Understanding:** This involves trying to see life as it really is, not how we believe it is or want it to be, accepting that hardship is part and parcel of life. For example, when a child starts school, they need to understand that first they have to learn the routine of school, where things are, how to behave, and so on. They can't just get into the classroom and expect to know it all. When we understand that life will be hard, even frustrating at times, we can meet any difficulties that arise more openly and creatively.

* **Right Intention:** The Buddha teaches that, along with Right Understanding, we need to show wholehearted commitment and persistence in our intention to do something. At school, for example, a child needs to *intend* to learn for learning to be successful.

* **Right Speech:** How we talk to ourselves and other people can have an impact not only on our experience of life, but also on our confidence and trust in ourselves and others. Right Speech means to speak truthfully, compassionately and considerately at all times.

* **Right Action:** This means treating others and everything around us as we would like ourselves and our belongings to be treated. So, for example, being kind and generous to classmates and looking after each other's and the school's property all follow the path of Right Action.

* **Right Livelihood:** For adults, this means being aware of the impact of our work on the environment and others. For children it's about

undertaking everything they do, whether school work or pastimes, with care and consideration, ensuring that they don't negatively impact on other people or their surroundings. The Buddha taught that a lack of respect for life in our work or play is a barrier to progress on the path to Enlightenment.

★ **Right Effort:** Applying ourselves to tasks with patience, care and attention makes a positive outcome more likely. If we are tense, slapdash, impatient or obsessive in our work, we are more likely to make mistakes and our efforts will be fruitless. The aim is to cultivate an attitude of steady and cheerful determination in everything we do. Children often throw themselves into tasks with great enthusiasm but then quickly become frustrated. Remind them to slow down and take their time!

★ **Right Mindfulness:** Whatever we do, at any age, our minds can easily get distracted. It's completely normal and natural for the mind to wander. However, when the mind does this, we are not inhabiting the present moment, fully appreciating all that moment has to offer. The Buddha teaches that the path to true inner peace requires complete focus in the present, rather than looking backward or forward. So, for example, a child who is opening a gift on their birthday would be better giving all their attention to that one act, rather than eagerly anticipating opening the next gift, or thinking about what they received in the last one, or the piece of cake they just ate.

★ **Right Concentration:** If our attention is not distracted, we can really focus on everything we do. In this way, we become more fully attuned to ourselves and the world around us – we experience a sense

of being at one with the world. No doubt you will have seen this when your child is calmly caught up in a favourite hobby.

The themes and guidelines of the Four Noble Truths and the Noble Eightfold Path provide the backbone for the stories in this book. Each story presents different dilemmas and solutions in a way that prepares young listeners to meet these challenges in their own lives. For example, in "The Bear Who Learned to Wait", Toby realizes that the way things are is the way things are – when he can't change the weather, he has to wait until nature brings him what he needs. In "The Singing Canary", we meet Mack, a plain, brown bird who is jealous of a beautiful, yellow canary with a glorious song. Mack's envy leads him to treat Apollo the canary unkindly, but the canary's gentle and honest response to that unkindness humbles Mack. He realizes that he should be thankful for the blessings he has, because everything is not always as it first seems. In "The Spoilt Prince", Prince Percival is given every toy, item of clothing or sweet treat he ever asks for. Yet, he doesn't find happiness until all his possessions are washed away and he learns the simple pleasures of compassion and companionship.

By deepening your child's understanding of the ways of Buddhism, even within the subtlety of this kind of storytelling, we encourage the practice of positive qualities, such as patience, kindness, love and gentle, humble self-confidence. And by using the stories and morals as a point of focus, we provide a gateway to that elusive downtime and, ultimately, to deep, restorative sleep.

The Wisdom in Storytelling

Children love listening to a story at bedtime. Not only does the cosy ritual of reading a story nurture parent–child bonds, but there is also evidence that it helps to develop children's brains, boosting their logic skills, expanding their vocabulary and firing up their imagination and creativity. It is such a lovely way to have fun together, relax and explore new ideas, concepts and values. Plus it provides a much-needed antidote to the sensory overload of technology and media exposure for adults and children alike.

The tradition of storytelling for both entertainment and education transcends culture. Although the eighteen stories in this book have been chosen from the Buddhist tradition, the values they seek to promote, such as compassion, wisdom, perseverance, generosity and patience, are timeless and borderless. They have been inspired by and adapted from a body of ancient Buddhist stories known as the Jataka Tales, which the Buddha himself is said to have told to pass on the many lessons he learned on his journey to peace and happiness. My hope is that my retellings convey the spirit and meaning of the original stories in a way that feels both accessible and relevant to the children of today.

While the tales can, of course, simply be read as fun stories, it is worth encouraging your child to engage more deeply with them when the time feels right, perhaps by pausing for reflection, asking questions and, of course, exploring the details of the artworks. Try thinking about the ways in which each tale's value applies specifically to your interactions as a family and to your child's own experiences.

I hope that engaging with the trials and successes of the characters in their different contemporary settings will give children insight into how to face some of the tricky experiences they might encounter growing up today. For example, bullying is explored in the story of "The Sweet-Tooth Charm"; sibling rivalry occurs in "Bethany's Bicycle". And both these two stories and others, such as "The Teddy Bear Tussle", touch on the issue of wanting something that's not ours – a common experience among children (and adults too).

From a Buddhist perspective, one of the most important lessons a child can learn is that all actions have consequences – and this is a theme explored in all the stories. Once a child understands this, they will have the ability to think and feel more fully before they act or speak. Ultimately, the underlying message of this book is that we all have control over our own destiny, no matter what age we are.

I hope that the tales in the pages that follow will help your child begin to develop a moral and ethical code that will empower them to grow into happy, compassionate and fulfilled human beings.

What is Mindfulness?

Mindfulness is a quality of gentle attention that we can bring to our moment-to-moment experience at any time we choose in order to help us feel more engaged, fulfilled and calm. It is the ability to be open and present to what is actually happening, as we really are, whether we are walking, eating, playing, reading a story or even trying to get to sleep. For children this means encouraging them to let their attention settle on a single chosen object or activity and to become fully absorbed in it. Psychologists today contend that being mindful can increase a child's "flourishing", making it easier for a child to:

* gain greater appreciation of and enjoyment from what they do
* adopt a sense of calm and quiet contemplation
* deal with difficulties and anxieties in their lives
* respond to desires with compassion, not frustration or anger
* tune in more deeply to others' feelings and build deeper relationships
* compromise, arbitrate and solve problems
* develop the self-confidence to accept themselves just as they are.

You can be mindful about pretty much anything. As you go about your daily routine, encourage your child to focus fully on what is happening – brushing their teeth, getting dressed, eating dinner and so on. You start by asking a question, such as: "Can you feel the bristles of the toothbrush on your gums?" "What does that sweater feel like on your skin? How is that different to your raincoat?" And, for example, when you are eating cake together, encourage your child to really take their time, to taste it and enjoy the texture, too. Eventually, with practice, your child will begin to notice these sensations more for themselves.

Some experts believe that mindfulness works, in part, by helping people to simply accept their experiences (including painful emotions) rather than reacting to them angrily or turning away and ignoring them. As children grow and face new challenges, mindfulness will remain a skill that can help them build their confidence, cope with stress calmly and constructively, and cultivate increased inner wisdom. Being more mindful also involves learning to be non-judgemental and compassionate toward whatever arises in our moment-to-moment experience. This kind, non-judgemental attitude is the foundation of emotional intelligence, healthy social relationships and sound mental health throughout life.

The stories in this book encourage mindfulness in both your children and yourselves, the parents. As you prepare your child for bedtime, one or both of you may become completely distracted (what parent hasn't hurried through bedtime in anticipation of their own quiet time?). Choosing a story starts the process of not only catching your child's attention – but also of catching yours. With gentle encouragement and patience, as you focus on the illustrations, find Archie and engage with the characters in each story, your child's mind and body will soon become more peaceful. And so will yours.

Percy Wins the Prize

Take a deep, relaxing breath, snuggle down and listen carefully to this tale about an ostrich called Percy who was fed up with not being able to see very well. He never knew where he was going and his knees were bruised from bumping into things. One day, all that changed. What do you think happened? Let's read the story and find out.

One morning, Percy was walking through the forest. He was thinking about the village fair and how he longed to win the running race. "But it's no good," he sighed, "I will just bump into everything." Just as he was thinking that, he almost stepped on a quail's nest!

"Look out, you long-legged fool! You nearly trod on my eggs," squawked Mrs Quail. She flapped her feathers and flew up into Percy's face. "Shoo!"

"What's going on?!" he cried in surprise and ran away. Wallop! Poor Percy ran straight into a tree. "Ouch!" he said. His knees crumpled and he slid to the ground in a daze. He began to cry. Tears flowed down his beak and plopped onto the ground in a big puddle.

"Please stop crying. You're going to drown me," muttered a tiny voice at Percy's feet.

Percy gulped back his tears and rubbed his eyes. He lowered his head, screwed up his nose and squinted at the ground. He could just make out a bright, rainbow-coloured shell. Two twinkling blue eyes on long stalks stared up at him.

"Hello. I'm Kevin," said the snail, and one twinkly blue eye winked at Percy. "Why are you crying?"

By now, he had climbed up onto Percy's foot, out of the puddle of tears.

Percy broke into sobs again. "Oh, Kevin," he said, "I want to win the running race at the village fair. I have the fastest legs for miles around."

"Lucky you!" said Kevin kindly. "I can't run fast. I don't have any legs." He wiggled his squishy body and laughed.

"But my fast legs are no use," said Percy. "Not really. My eyesight is so bad I can't see where I'm going."

"Oh dear," said Kevin. "I wonder what can be done?" He was a clever little snail and believed every problem has a solution. So he sat and thought. "I know," he said at last. "I could be your eyes. I have excellent eyesight. I'll sit on your head and tell you where you're going."

"Really?" said Percy. "You would help me like that?"

"Of course I would!" said Kevin. He was already slithering up toward the top of Percy's head. "I would very much enjoy a fast ride. Let's have a practice now."

"All right," said Percy, and as soon as Kevin was settled, Percy began to run.

"Whee!" cried Kevin as they thundered along the path. "Just look out for that tree on the left." Percy swerved out of the way. "And Mrs Quail's nest is just in front of you," warned Kevin. Percy darted sideways, away from the precious eggs.

"Thank you for being so careful!" cried Mrs Quail.

"Whoopee!" cried Percy, and he ran on faster than ever.

Percy was ecstatic! He told Kevin there was a whole week until the big race. The two friends practised every day, enjoying lots of chatting and laughter as they did so.

The other animals watched in wonder as Percy sped about, leaving a trail of dust behind him. "Look how fast I can run," he boasted. "I'm going to win first prize!"

"We are going to win together," said Kevin in his tiny voice. But Percy took no notice, he just kept on practising, with Kevin showing him the way. Soon Percy didn't bother even to say "good morning" to Kevin when they met to practise, and he never said "thank you" when they were finished each night.

Instead, he just blurted out instructions. "Hurry up and tell me where to go," he ordered the little snail.

"Turn left," said Kevin quietly. "And look out for the fallen tree trunk." He was sad that Percy had started ordering him around in this way.

On the morning of the village fair, Kevin tried to tell Percy how he was feeling. "I thought we were a team," he said. But the big bird just snapped his beak. "Stop moaning. You're lucky you get to ride with me at all. Today is the big race and I am going to win the prize."

"We will win it together," said Kevin again as Percy took his place with the other runners on the starting line.

"Oh, do be quiet! If it wasn't for me you'd still be living under a rock," scolded Percy. "I am fast. I am a winner. I am the best of the best. You are not fast. You are not …"

But Kevin wasn't listening any more. He'd had enough. While the ostrich was bragging, and without saying a word, Kevin had climbed onto a leaf and disappeared into the bushes, leaving boastful Percy to race alone.

BANG! The starting gun sounded and the race began.

Percy started to run, but without Kevin's help, he couldn't see where he was going. "Kevin! Where are you?" he squawked. All he could see was a fuzzy mist. He tripped over his own feet and landed in a heap in the thick bushes. The other runners sped away.

24

"Oh dear," he said, untangling his feathers from a particularly prickly bush. "I've been a very silly ostrich. I'll never win the race now." Then he started to cry. But it wasn't losing the race that made him sad – it was the thought that he had lost his friendship with Kevin.

"Excuse me. Can you please stop crying," said a voice below him, "or I am going to drown."

Percy squinted at the ground. "Kevin!" he cried. "I'm sorry I was so mean, especially when you were so kind to me." He hung his head in shame. "We were a team."

"Yes," said Kevin, "we were." Then, seeing Percy was truly sorry, he said, "Thank you for realizing how bad you made me feel. I forgive you. Can we be friends again?"

"Yes, please! Friends!" agreed Percy, and Kevin climbed up onto Percy's head.

As they began to walk away together, Kevin said: "I'm sorry that you didn't win the race. Perhaps we can have another go next year. You can try to win the prize then."

"That would be fun," agreed Percy. "But the thing that matters most is that you and I are friends again."

True friendship is precious and should never be taken for granted. A wise person knows that a good friend is the greatest prize that can be won.

The Gentle Dragon

Take a deep, relaxing breath, snuggle down and listen carefully to this tale about a gentle dragon who was cruelly taken captive. Do you think he managed to escape? Let's read the story and find out.

There once was a mighty dragon who could breathe fire hotter than a volcano. His claws were as sharp as daggers and the spikes on his back were like the blades of an axe. Yet the dragon was a peaceful soul. He lived quietly in a deep cave on a mountainside. On sunny days he dozed in a hillside meadow, keeping far away from the people living in the towns and villages below.

One day, a prince came riding through the meadow, and saw the dozing dragon. "Seize the beast!" he cried to his huntsmen. "And take him back to the castle!"

The huntsmen jabbed at the dragon with their spears. "Come on, you great brute," they roared.

The dragon knew that with one puff of his fiery breath, he could burn them all to cinders. But he also knew that if he did, more men would come, and they would hunt him till the end of time. So, he did not fight. He let the men push and prod and poke him all the way to the castle, where they tied him up in a net in the castle courtyard.

"Tomorrow I will slay you in the market square," boasted the prince. The dragon simply looked away.

Then, as darkness fell, the dragon used the blades on his tail to cut the net. And with a swoosh of his mighty wings, he flew back to his cave to sleep.

Next morning, the prince was livid. He gathered his huntsmen and marched back to the meadow. This time they had whips as well as spears. They caught the dragon and dragged him back to the castle courtyard, tying him up in chains. "Show us your fire now!" the prince goaded.

"I don't want to fight," said the dragon simply.

"Then tomorrow," sneered the prince, "you will die."

But that night, with one fiery puff, the dragon melted the chains and then he flew home to sleep in his cave.

On the third day the prince and the huntsmen came again. This time they had flaming torches, and they threw the dragon into the deepest dungeon.

"You can never escape now," laughed the prince. "Tomorrow I will slay you!" But the dragon picked the lock on the dungeon door with the tip of his claw and tiptoed past the sleeping guard as quietly as a kitten.

28

This time he'd had enough. "If the prince insists on turning me out of my own bed, then I shall sleep in his!" he thought. He crept up the castle stairs and into the prince's room, where he lay at the foot of his bed and waited for him to wake up. When the prince opened his eyes, he was too scared to call for help. "Don't hurt me!" he trembled.

"One puff of my fiery breath and you'd be dead," said the dragon calmly. "But I don't want to harm you. Many men and dragons have died fighting one another. I want only to live quietly in my cave on the mountain. I will spare your life, but will you leave me to live as I please?"

The prince was humbled. He realized that the dragon was right. So many of his aunts and uncles had died fighting dragons. Surely it would be better to live side by side. "Go in peace!" he said. "I will not trouble you again."

"Thank you!" breathed the dragon. And he flapped his wings and flew out through the prince's open window – to live happily in his cave on the mountain for evermore.

Being nasty when someone else is mean only fills the world with meanness. A wise person knows that a benevolent and gentle response always works best.

Cornflower the Mischievous Donkey

Take a deep, relaxing breath, snuggle down and listen carefully to this tale about a mischievous donkey called Cornflower, who thought she was very clever and very funny. She loved to play tricks on people, but sometimes she couldn't help taking things just a little too far. Do you think her tricks eventually got her into trouble? Let's read the story and find out.

Late one afternoon, Cornflower was peeping through a gap in a hedge and giggling quietly to herself. She had just nibbled a big hole in Ms Cherry's shopping bag while she was talking to Mrs O'Connor, the farmer's wife. Flour was spilling from Ms Cherry's bag like snow, but neither of the women had noticed a thing.

Just then a big gust of wind blew along the lane. It threw the flour up into the air, where it hung for a moment in a cloud and then dropped down covering the two women from head to toe. Smothered in the white flour, they spluttered in surprise. Cornflower had to bite her lip so as not to burst out laughing and give herself away. She ducked her head behind the hedge and retreated. When she was safely out of earshot, she burst into wild hee-haws. She rolled on the ground, laughing so much that tears streamed down her long cheeks. After a while her laughter settled down to a few random snorts. "Being me is too much fun!" she giggled, delighted with herself.

By the time Cornflower had got over her laughter, it was getting dark. She scrambled up and hurried home toward her nice, warm stable on Mr and Mrs O'Connor's farm. She was trotting down the lane when a big, white shadow suddenly blew through the trees in front of her. She froze on the spot and brayed with fright.

"It's a ghoul!" she cried. The ghostly shape hovered above her and then dropped to the ground right in front of Cornflower. She shivered as she stared down at it, too scared to move. Then the moon came out from behind the trees, casting its light on the ground, and Cornflower saw there was no ghost at all!

"You silly old donkey, it's just a harmless sheet!" she laughed. "It must have blown off Mrs O'Connor's washing line." But then she had an idea. "What a marvellous prank it could be to scare everybody with this sheet! I could disguise myself as a ghost and give everyone I meet a real fright."

Cornflower picked up the sheet with her big teeth, tossed back her head and threw the sheet over herself so it covered her all the way down to her hooves. She bit two eye-holes in the fabric so she could see where she was going, then trotted off to see who she could spook.

She startled the chickens and the ducks. She rattled the dog and the sheep. She frightened the cat and the cows. And she terrified poor Ms Cherry. Soon the evening air was alive with clucking, quacking, barking, bleating, screeching, mooing and screaming, as Cornflower slipped in and out of barns and meadows, past pens and hutches, sending animals and people fleeing in every direction. Cornflower had so much fun scaring everybody that she dressed up in the sheet again the following night. And the night after that. Soon word spread that there was a fiendish ghost haunting the barns, fields and lanes around the farm.

One evening, Mrs O'Connor was sitting in her cosy kitchen stroking Truffles the cat, while her husband told her all the tales of the strange sightings.

"Goodness!" she cried. "Perhaps it was the ghost who covered me in flour!"

Just then, she saw something white outside the window and jumped up. Truffles went flying through the air and landed on Mr O'Connor's head. "Heavens! It's

– it's … the ghost!" stammered Mrs O'Connor, pointing at the kitchen window. Then she fainted. Her husband, meanwhile, banged around the kitchen trying to pry the terrified Truffles from his head.

"Oh, how hilarious!" said Cornflower under her breath as she pressed her sheet-covered nose against the kitchen window, watching the pandemonium inside. She found the whole thing so funny that she couldn't contain herself any longer and accidentally let out a very loud hee-haw.

The sound of the donkey's braying stopped Mr O'Connor in his tracks and roused Mrs O'Connor from her faint. They all turned and looked toward the window.

"A ghost, indeed!" cried Mrs O'Connor. "It's that rascal donkey Cornflower playing tricks again! I would recognize that braying anywhere!"

She jumped up from the kitchen floor and flew to the door, followed closely by her husband, who now had Truffles clinging to his shoulder.

"CORNFLOWER!" bellowed Mr O'Connor. "We know it's you under that sheet!"

Terrified at the thought of what would happen if they caught her, Cornflower started to run. But her hooves caught in the sheet and she fell into the duck pond with a great SPLASH! Now it was Mr and Mrs O'Connor's turn to

34

laugh – and Truffles and the ducks, too! There in the moonlight was Cornflower, the white sheet still clinging to her back. She was stuck in the middle of the muddy pond, soaking wet and covered in weeds and slime.

"Quack! Quack! Quack!" The ducks laughed so hard they thought they would burst. The sound of their laughter, and of the guffaws from Mr and Mrs O'Connor and Truffles, soon woke the cows and the sheep and the dog – and even Ms Cherry next door. Everyone came to see what all the noise was about. When they saw Cornflower sitting in the pond in her soggy sheet, they laughed too.

"That's what you get for playing tricks on people, you naughty donkey!" said Mr O'Connor as Cornflower finally scrambled out of the pond, her head hanging in shame.

"I'm so sorry," she muttered, as she trotted home to her warm, dry stable, promising never to play tricks again.

Actions have consequences. A wise person knows that those who try to make a fool of others may end up making an even greater fool of themselves.

The Sweet-Tooth Charm

Take a deep, relaxing breath, snuggle down and listen carefully to this tale about Bobby, a boy who was training to be a wizard. One day, he got into big trouble on his way home from Wiz School. What do you think went wrong? Let's read the story and find out.

One chilly afternoon, Bobby was hurrying along the snowy mountain path back to his home in the valley. He had just learned a new spell at Wiz School and wanted to give all his friends in the village a wonderful surprise.

He was whistling merrily to himself. His Wiz School cloak hung snugly around his shoulders, and his hands were thrust deep in his pockets to protect them from the cold. In his right pocket, he could feel the smooth surface of the sugary charm he had made that day in class. It was a Sweet-Tooth Charm full of special magic. As soon as he was with his friends, he would say the magic words and the charm would fizz and crackle and make the most delicious candies appear from nowhere: Red Roarers that whistle when you suck, Orange Swirly Pops that make your tongue stripy, Fiery Flashes that fizz in your mouth, Green Globes that turn into gum and make your tongue go green, Rainbow Snakes that crackle with popping candy, Strawberry Delights filled with soft cream, and Spider Saucers that are sweet and sour all at once. Bobby couldn't wait for his friends to try all the treats.

He was so excited that he didn't notice two boys creeping up behind him. Before he knew it, the bullies had grabbed the collar of his cloak and lifted his feet off the ground.

"Give us some money!" they demanded.

"I don't have any money!" said Bobby. "But I *can* do *magic*!" he stammered. "Really?" asked the boys.

"Yes, I have a charm in my pocket, but it will only work once, so if you come with me to the village, I'll make candies rain from the sky!"

The boys dropped Bobby back onto his feet. "What sort of candies?" they asked suspiciously.

"Fiery Flashes, Green Globes, Spider Saucers ..." said Bobby. "All the really good ones. There will be enough for everyone to share."

"No way!" said one bully. "We don't share. Magic up the treats here and now!" He twisted Bobby's ear, while the other boy pinched his nose.

"Stop!" Bobby pleaded. "If you let me go, I'll do the spell now." He was almost crying. His nose stung and his ear hurt, and he was sad not to be able to share the delicious sweets with his friends. He took a deep breath, reached inside his pocket for the charm and then held up his wand. "Nimby numby, flum tiddle tum," he muttered, waving his wand over the Sweet-Tooth Charm. "Make sugary swirls and candy curls come." The charm began to fizz and crackle. Then it shot up into the air like a firework. There was a loud BANG! and a shower of brightly coloured sweets rained down on the path.

"Wow!" The bullies opened their mouths wide to catch the falling treasure. But they couldn't catch anywhere near as many as they wanted. "Give us your dumb cape!" they cried, pushing Bobby to the ground and pulling his Wiz School cloak off his arms. They held out the cloak to catch the falling sweets. Then they scurried away with their mouths full and the cloak bulging with goodies.

Bobby staggered to his feet and stared helplessly down the path after them. "Now I can't surprise my friends. And I've lost my school cloak, too."

But, before the bullies could get very far, a gang of four big boys came the other way. They had seen the boys catching the falling sweets. "Give us that!" the gang leader barked, pointing at the cloak.

"No! These candies are ours. We're not sharing them. Go and get your own!" They pointed back toward where Bobby had been standing on the path. "That boy Bobby, over there. He can make sweets rain from the sky."

The leader of the gang marched in the direction the boys were pointing. He couldn't see Bobby, who had hidden behind a tree. "He's gone!" shouted the gang leader. "Now stop talking and give us what's in that cloak!" The gang closed in on the two bullies.

"No way!" shouted the bullies, and a terrible fight broke out. The bigger boys punched the smaller ones; and the smaller boys kicked the bigger ones.

Bobby shuddered at the noises of the fight, but peeping out from his hiding place, he saw that in all the commotion the bullies had dropped the cloak full of sweets on the ground. It was little more than an arm's reach away from him. Quick as a flash, he darted forward, grabbed the cloak and ran helter-skelter down the mountain path.

"Hurry!" he called, shouting to his friends as he ran into the snowy streets of the village. "Tell everyone to come to the market square. I've got candies for everyone." All the village children ran out of their houses and Bobby laid his cloak on the ground.

"Help yourselves!" he said. And everybody did. There were plenty of sweets to go around. Soon all the village children had green tongues from chewing the Green Globes. They gasped in delight as the Rainbow Snakes crackled and popped on their tongues and the Fiery Flashes fizzed in their mouths. "Yum!" they all said. "Thank you, Bobby. These are the best sweets ever!"

Meanwhile, up on the mountain, the two gangs of boys had realized the sweets had gone. "What are we even fighting over?" asked one of them.

Bruised and battered, they limped down the mountain. In the village, all the children had their hands full of sweets. Embarrassed, the bullies slunk off as Bobby ran toward them. "Hey, wait!" he called. "I've got something for you." He pulled out a handful of sweets. "I saved some for you, seeing as you wanted them so badly." The boys could not believe their eyes, and Bobby's generosity made them feel ashamed at their own greediness.

"We're sorry we tried to bully you," said the gang leader. "Thanks, Bobby," they all said. "Maybe you could teach us how to do that charm? Then we can make sweets for the whole village too!"

When we are selfish and greedy, we risk losing everything. A wise person shares with an open heart, and enjoys plenty for themselves in return.

The Monster
Who Came to Tea

Take a deep, relaxing breath, snuggle down and listen carefully to this tale about five children who spent the summer with their aunt who lived deep inside a great wood. One day the children decided to play at being explorers, but they didn't like what they found. What do you think that was? Let's read the story and find out.

It was a beautiful, sunny afternoon and the children asked if they could go outside to play.

"Of course. Just don't go too far," Aunt Dotti warned, "tea won't be long."

But Freddy, Molly, Ginger, Trolly and little Nutt (the youngest) were already zooming up and down the lawn chasing each other. Freddy, who was the eldest, found a ball in the shrubbery and called for a game of catch.

The children were having a wonderful time until Freddy threw the ball so high it flew above the other children's outstretched fingers. It whizzed out of the garden and into the dark wood beyond.

"We had better go and fetch it," sighed Molly.

Little Nutt wasn't sure that was a good idea. She didn't like the look of those tall, scary trees. "Auntie said not to go far," she reminded them. "There could be monsters!"

"Don't worry! I'll look after you," said Freddy, scooping her up onto his shoulders.

"Let's imagine we're explorers deep in the jungle," said Ginger.

"In search of ancient treasure," added Molly.

"Come on, then," called Freddy, leading the children away from the cottage.

"It's spooky in here," whispered Nutt as they made their way further into the forest.

"What was that?" squeaked Trolly, grabbing Ginger's arm as something squawked overhead.

"Just a bird," said Ginger reassuringly, trying not to sound scared himself.

"I don't like this, I want to go back!" said Trolly.

"Just a bit further. This is excit …" But Freddy's voice trailed off. Something very large was crashing through the trees toward them. The children stared at each other.

"Run!" shouted Freddy, and they all scattered in different directions. Freddy, who was still carrying Nutt, crouched behind the nearest bush. The ground shook.

"I knew there'd be monsters in here," whimpered Nutt.

"Shhh!" whispered Freddy. He lifted Nutt so that she could peer round the bush. She caught sight of a huge log-like monster thumping down on the ground and clamped her hands over her mouth so as not to scream.

Freddy looked up. He saw a long, grey snake waving its head high above him and yelled a warning: "A snake! A snake!"

Meanwhile, Molly had climbed into a tree. She held her breath and peeked round the tree trunk. She saw a big, greenish-brown eye staring at her.

"A monster!" she screeched. She was so surprised she fell out of the tree and landed deep in the soft undergrowth.

"Hreee-uh!" roared the monster.

Aunt Dotti was just taking a cake out the oven for tea. Hearing the noise, she turned her head and looked up.

"That's Mr Titch," she said to herself. "I must introduce him to the children." Then she went back to her cake.

Meanwhile, Ginger was shaking with fright. He had heard the "Hreee-uh!" too and hidden behind a bush. His body was hidden but his legs stuck out. A big, slobbery thing rolled over them – a slug-like grey tongue was licking his legs! Then off it slurped, leaving his knees covered in glistening slime. "Yuk!" he squealed.

Trolly hid beside a tree trunk as the thing lumbered away into the shadows. As soon as it was out of

sight, he jumped down. "It's a huge boulder," he said, "crushing everything in its path!"

Back in the kitchen, Aunt Dotti had just finished decorating her cake with strawberries. She put it on a plate and carried it into the garden. "Come on, children!" she hollered.

Relieved to hear their aunt, they crashed through the trees toward her voice. "Help! A monster!"

"A monster?" said Aunt Dotti in surprise.

"It was a massive, slimy slug," said Ginger.

"It was an alien with a big, brown eye," insisted Molly.

"It was like a giant boulder, rolling through the wood and crushing everything in its path," argued Trolly.

"No! It was the biggest snake ever," cried Freddy.

"It was a huge grey log monster!" piped up little Nutt.

"Hmm!" Aunt Dotti tried to speak, but she was drowned out by the clamour of arguing children. Finally, when no one could hear what anyone was saying because everyone was shouting at the same time, Aunt Dotti whistled very loudly. The children fell silent.

"What if *each* of you is right?" Aunt Dotti asked.

"We can't all be right! There must have been five monsters," said Ginger, glancing warily at the trees.

"Let's think," said Aunt Dotti. "What would you get if you made all five of your monsters into one big one?"

The children shuddered at the thought of the terrifying monster that would make, but Aunt Dotti laughed.

"Look!" she said, pointing toward the wood.

The children turned and gasped. A wrinkly, grey elephant was rolling through the trees on his big, stumpy feet. His brown eyes sparkled like gemstones and his slippery tongue lolled out of his mouth as he rumbled along like a boulder, happily swinging his long trunk.

"I'd like you to meet my old friend Mr Titch," beamed Aunt Dotti. "I should have warned you, he always wanders over from the circus on the other side of the wood when he smells me baking cakes!"

"Hreee-uh!" said Mr Titch in agreement.

"We were *all* right!" laughed Freddy. "We each saw different parts of Mr Titch!"

"I'm sorry," said Molly. "I should have listened to you."

"We should have listened to each other," said Ginger.

"At least he's not a real monster," whispered Nutt.

"Hreee-uh!" said the elephant, and he picked up a slice of Aunt Dotti's cake with his trunk and ate it in one gulp.

It's important to listen to other people's opinions. A wise person knows we need to consider other viewpoints as well as our own to discover the truth.

Crystal and the Pixie

Take a deep, relaxing breath, snuggle down and listen carefully to this tale about a little girl called Crystal. One day, she had an extraordinary adventure. What do you think happened? Let's read the story and find out.

Crystal's head had been thumping for two whole days and she felt hot and shivery all over. "It's not fair!" she croaked. "I want to go to Gloria's party this afternoon."

"I'm sorry, sweetheart. You're not well enough," said Dad. "You need to stay in bed for another day, at least."

Crystal burst into tears. She'd been looking forward to the party so much. "Gloria's my best friend and I wanted to wear my lovely new dress," she sobbed.

"I know," said Dad as he plumped her pillow. "But just try to rest. Perhaps you'll feel brighter after that." Tears ran down Crystal's hot cheeks, but soon she fell asleep.

And as she slept she had the strangest dream …

A pixie in a rainbow-coloured waistcoat floated toward her on a cloud. "Don't cry!" he said kindly, and he patted the cloud so that Crystal could sit beside him. "Sometimes it helps to talk to someone about your problems. Do you want to tell me what's up?"

In the dream, Crystal was wearing her beautiful new party dress. The little pixie seemed very kind, so Crystal snuffled back her tears and told him everything: "I have a sore head and my tummy hurts. I can't stop crying because it's my best friend's party and Dad says I can't go. I have to stay in bed and it's just not fair! I'm going to be in bed for the rest of my life, I know it!" As she talked, tears started rolling down her cheeks again.

"Oh dear! It's a good job I'm a magic pixie," he said. "I'm sure I can make you feel better."

"What do you mean?" said Crystal curiously. "Can you grant three magic wishes …?"

The pixie smiled. "Something like that. What would you wish for?"

"That's easy!" said Crystal, holding up her fingers. "One, I wish I wasn't ill. Two, I wish I didn't feel so upset. And three … I wish I could go to the party!"

Without a moment's hesitation, the pixie said: "Well, all you have to do is find a handkerchief to dry those tears."

"Is that all?" asked Crystal. This really was a wonderful dream. "If I find a hanky, my wishes will come true?"

"Yes!" the pixie nodded. "But you have to get the hanky from someone who has never felt upset, sick or hurt – someone who has never cried."

"I can do that! That's easy!" said Crystal, hopping onto a rainbow at the edge of the cloud. She slid down it like a slide. "Dad is the bravest man alive and Mum is never ill. I bet neither of them ever cries. Grown-ups don't cry."

Crystal peered in through her living room window. Mum was passing Dad a tissue. They were watching a sad movie on TV and they were both crying. For a moment Crystal was upset she couldn't get her hanky from them, then she had an idea. "I know! I'll phone Uncle Theo instead. He's a police officer, so I bet he's never cried!"

A jolly-looking sunflower appeared and passed Crystal a phone. But when she called up Uncle Theo, he told her he did sometimes cry – like when his son Blue went off to college and he missed him. So she racked her brains to figure out who else she could phone.

One by one, she tried them. Aunt Jenny, the firefighter; Cousin Peter, who was studying to be a nurse; and even Miss Ingram, her teacher. But they all told her about times in their lives when they'd felt so hurt or upset that they'd cried. Finally, Crystal spotted Grandpa. He was floating past on a cloud, merrily waving his walking stick at her.

"Hi there!" she called. Surely Grandpa was far too wise to cry. But even he said he got sad and frustrated enough to cry at times, like when Grandma Josephine had passed away, or his arthritis got very painful.

"I try to let myself be upset for only a little while though," he said, kissing her as he floated away. "You know, sadness is part of life."

"Any luck finding that handkerchief?" said the little pixie, sliding down the rainbow to join her.

Crystal shook her head. "I can't find anyone who has never been upset, sick or hurt. Even the grown-ups!"

"You see, Crystal, everybody hurts and cries at times," said the pixie. "The important thing to remember is that sadness and disappointment will pass. If you have to miss a party, it's not the end of the world. Think about something fun you and your friend can do together to celebrate her birthday when you feel better instead."

Crystal nodded. "Maybe Gloria and I can have a special party of our own with our favourite cake," she said. "I could even still wear my lovely new dress."

"Exactly," said the pixie. But he was starting to fade away in a swirl of colours. The next thing Crystal knew, Dad was offering her a drink of water as she woke up.

"You slept for a long time," he said as she sat up to take the drink. "Do you feel any better?"

"A bit," said Crystal, stretching. "I had a weird dream." Then she looked at her father strangely. "Dad, do you ever cry at things you see on TV?"

"Like a baby!" Dad blushed. "There's an old black-and-white movie that Mum and I love, but it always makes us cry! We get through a box of tissues when we watch it." Crystal squeezed his hand. "To tell the truth, I often feel better after a good cry!" said Dad.

"I know what you mean," agreed Crystal. "I'm still sad to miss Gloria's party, but I know this feeling won't last for ever. It's like that wise pixie said, nothing lasts for ever. I'll stop feeling ill soon, and I know I'll stop feeling sad, too."

"That's very true," said Dad. "Clever girl." But he scratched his head. "What wise pixie?"

Crystal laughed. "Oh, just a new friend I met in my dream. We had a real adventure. Sit down and I'll tell you all about it." And, feeling much better already, that's exactly what she did.

We all feel upset from time to time — that's part of life. A wise person remembers that the sadness will pass and happier times will come again.

The Bear Who Learned to Wait

Take a deep, relaxing breath, snuggle down and listen carefully to this tale about a bear who set out to find himself a new home. Where do you think he ended up living? Let's read the story and find out.

Deep in the heart of an emerald forest grew a great fig tree. Its branches brimmed with delicious fruit and luscious leaves that provided food and shelter for the many animals that made the tree their home.

One day, a young brown bear called Toby passed by. He had grown too big to live with his parents in their cave anymore, so he had left the mountains in search of a new home of his own.

The moment he saw the lush, green fig tree, he knew it would make the perfect home. "This is the place!" he said to himself, scratching his back on the knobbly trunk. The thick, tangled leaves gave plenty of shade for him to nap in when the sun was fierce, and the branches bore all the fruit a small bear could ever need to fill his tummy.

"Welcome!" squawked a clever, brightly coloured parrot called Pip, who lived in the branches above. She perched on Toby's shoulder and asked him all about his mum and dad and the cave where he used to live. As the days passed, Pip told him about her many adventures flying through the forest. Soon, the two were the best of friends and Toby was never lonely. He was very happy indeed with his lovely new home.

Then, after Toby had lived beneath the tree for some months, he noticed a change. The leaves began to fall and the fruit started to shrivel up. One morning, he woke up very hot and bothered. The branches above him were almost totally bare, and the bright sun was pouring down onto his fur making him far too warm to sleep.

"What has happened?" he asked as Pip fluttered down from the bare branches. "Is our tree dying?"

"The tree is thirsty," Pip replied. "We have to wait for the rains to come, then the leaves will grow back and you'll have all your shade again."

But Toby wanted his shade back straight away. "I can't stay here!" he wailed. "It was never this hot in my parents' cave. I need to be cool!" He stomped off down the forest path. A little way off he found a thorn bush. The branches were prickly, but there were quite a few leaves. "This will be my new home!" he said.

Toby tried to settle down under the thorn bush, but the leaves were too small to provide proper shade, and he was just as hot as he'd been beneath the fig tree. Even worse, the prickles caught in his fur. When Pip came to visit that night, she had to peck them out, one by one.

"Come back to the tree," she said, kindly. "It's your home. It won't be long before the rains arrive."

"Rains?" said Toby, glancing at the sky. "I don't see any rains." And off he went further down the path until he came across a hollow log.

"This will be my home now," he said. "I can crawl inside it and stay out of the sun." But the log was cramped. As he tried to sleep, squashed and uncomfortable, Toby realized he had no one to talk to. He missed Pip and all the other birds and animals who lived in the fig tree. "This is silly," he told himself. "Pip is right. I should just be patient and wait for the rain."

The next morning, he wandered back to the fig tree to visit his friends. Pip perched on his shoulder and, while they talked, she made Toby a beautiful broad-rimmed hat out of dry leaves to help keep her friend cool. But Toby soon became cross again. "It's no good!" he complained. "Even your clever hat can't keep me cool in this burning heat. I've had enough!" He leapt to his feet, sending poor Pip flying up into the air.

Toby stretched up his paws and grabbed the tree by a low branch. "Hurry up and grow leaves again," he shouted, tugging at the branch. But as he tugged, the whole branch cracked and came off in his paws.

"Careful!" cried Pip. "The tree is dry! You have to be patient. You can't hurry nature."

Toby knew he shouldn't have hurt the tree. He tossed the branch aside. "It's too hot here. I need a nap!" he said, and he trudged back to his lonely, cramped log.

He stayed in the log for what seemed a very long time. Some days Pip would visit him to tell him the news from the fig tree, but often Toby would just sit and wait, all alone. He thought the rains would never come. Then, one morning, he poked his head out of the log and felt something cold and wet land on the end of his nose – plop! It was a raindrop! Then … plop! plop! plop!

A clap of thunder echoed across the sky. The drops came faster until the rain was pouring down in torrents. Toby ran back to the fig tree. "Pip, you were right!" he cried. "The rains *have* come."

"You see!" Pip laughed, as they sheltered together in the roots of the fig tree. "You just had to be patient."

After several long, wet days, a thick, luscious canopy had grown like an umbrella above Toby's head.

But he still wasn't happy. "Pip!" he cried impatiently, on the fifth day of rain. "How long will this go on for?" His bed was wet and water kept plip-plopping through the twigs and branches above and trickling down his ears.

"Only a little longer." Pip ruffled her wet feathers. "If you can't wait, you can always go back to the prickly thorn bush or your lonely log," she teased.

"No way!" said Toby. "I'm staying here with you. You told me to be patient when it was hot and dry and you were right. You will probably be right this time, too!" He picked up the old sun hat Pip had made him and put it on his head to keep the rain off his nose.

Two days later the sun came out. The tree looked just as fresh and beautiful as it had on the very first day Toby had decided to make it his home. "Perfect!"

Toby sighed as he lay down and relaxed in the cool shade of the bright new leaves. Pip chattered away above his head. "I told you you needed to be patient!" she squawked, seeing how happy he was. "Yes," replied Toby, closing his eyes and smiling. "This is well worth the wait."

There's no point letting yourself get frustrated and impatient. A wise person knows that the good things in life are worth waiting for.

59

Bethany's Bicycle

Take a deep, relaxing breath, snuggle down and listen carefully to this tale about a girl called Bethany whose birthday present caused a lot of trouble. Why do you think that was? Let's read the story and find out.

Bethany had four older brothers and sisters, and they all lived together with their mother, father and grandfather. Most of Bethany's clothes and toys were hand-me-downs from her siblings. One day, just before her sixth birthday, Bethany's grandpa promised that she would get something special all of her own that year. And sure enough, when she came downstairs on the morning of her big day, she found an exciting parcel in the kitchen tied with an enormous red bow.

"Grandpa's busy working in the shed, but he says you should go right ahead and open your gift without him," said Dad.

Bethany tore open the paper to find the shiniest red bike she had ever seen. "Wow! Is it really mine?" she said.

"Of course," said Dad.

Bethany's brothers and sisters had been watching. "That's not fair," roared Paula, the eldest of the five children. "Why does she get a new bike? I don't have one."

"It's not your birthday," said Mum. "Now take Bethany to have a go on it outside and make sure you don't go near any cars."

But once they were outside, Gemma, Bethany's other big sister, grabbed the bike. "Red is my favourite colour and that means I should ride it first." Riley and Robbie, Bethany's twin brothers, pushed her out the way as they chased after Gemma.

"Wait!" cried Bethany, running as fast as she could after them all. "Grandpa gave it to *me* – I'd like to ride it first! You can have a turn afterwards," she said. But no one was listening.

"I bet I'm the fastest rider," said Riley.

"I bet I'm faster than you," said Robbie.

"Please," said Bethany. "Can I have a go?"

No one took any notice. Riley snatched the bike from Gemma, leapt on the saddle and whizzed off down the street with Robbie racing after him on foot.

"Come back!" she cried helplessly as they all pelted away. She had lost her present already.

"I'd better go and thank Grandpa, even if I never get to ride it," she sighed. She found Grandpa in his shed. He was always in there, making new things or mending old ones. "Happy birthday!" he cried as he saw her coming. "Do you like your surprise?"

"Oh yes!" said Bethany, "I love it!" But as she spoke her voice wobbled and her eyes filled with tears.

"What's wrong?" Grandpa put down his hammer.

Bethany burst into tears. "The others said it was unfair that I had something so special. They've all gone off with the bike. I want to share it with them but they won't even let me have a go."

"Oh, that's not right!" said Grandpa.

"Gemma says the bike should be hers because she loves red. The twins say it should be theirs because they're faster than me," she sobbed. "Paula says I'm spoilt …"

"Hmm! You're not spoilt at all. It's your birthday and you deserve that bike," said Grandpa. "They've all had nice presents from me on their own birthdays in the past … I know what to do."

Then, he told Bethany his clever idea. "With your help, I'll teach the others a bit of a lesson," he said as he headed out of the house and down the street.

He found the bike lying on the street corner, while Bethany's brothers and sisters stood nearby arguing over who should have the next go and who most deserved a new bike. He picked up the bike without any of them noticing, and carried it back to his shed.

That afternoon, after Bethany had blown out the candles on her cake and was happily scoffing a huge slice, Mum asked what had happened to her present.

"Well," said Bethany, "as everyone started fighting over it, Grandpa took it back."

"What a shame!" said Mum.

Bethany shrugged. "I'd rather have no bike than see everyone fighting over who should have it instead of me."

The other children had stopped talking and were staring down at their plates.

"Oh, don't worry," said Bethany. "Grandpa promised he'd make sure that by the end of the day, there would be no need for anyone to be jealous."

"Maybe we're *all* getting new bikes!" cried Paula.

Just then the kitchen door opened. Grandpa came in, struggling with five carefully wrapped parcels in his arms.

"One for each of you," he puffed. "Open them up."

The children grinned. But as they opened their parcels, their expressions fell. Gemma had handlebars. Paula had pedals. The twins each had a wheel. And Bethany had a bell. There was silence. "What's the matter?" said Grandpa. "Don't you like your presents? You all thought it was so unfair that Bethany got a brand-new bike all to herself, I thought I'd give you each a little piece of it."

The children looked sheepishly at Grandpa.

"Wheels are no use on their own," said Riley and Robbie together. "I can't ride just pedals," said Paula. "And my handlebars have nothing to steer," said Gemma. "Sorry for spoiling your birthday, Bethany," she said. One by one, they each placed the pieces of the bike at Bethany's feet.

"Please can you put my bike back together again, Grandpa?" she asked.

An hour later, Grandpa returned with the shiny, new bike, all put together again. "I'm afraid there's one thing missing," he said.

"What?" asked Bethany in dismay.

"That!" Grandpa smiled, pointing at the bell Bethany was holding. He attached it to the handlebars and handed over the bike. "Happy birthday!" he said.

"Thanks, Grandpa," said Bethany. "You can all have a turn in a minute," she said to her siblings. "But it's my go first!" And with a ding of her bell, off she pedalled.

Being jealous about someone else's possessions will only make us sad. A wise person knows to be grateful for what we have and to try to share it.

The Spoilt Prince

Take a deep, relaxing breath, snuggle down and listen carefully to this tale about a young prince who was given everything he ever wanted. How happy do you think he was? Let's read the story and find out.

Prince Percival was spoilt. "I want roller skates!" he would cry. And he would get them! If he asked for a golden rocking horse, he got one. If he asked for two golden rocking horses, he got both … and a ride-on train, a dartboard and a telescope too. And clothes, sweet treats, fancy gadgets – you name it, he got it.

The King and Queen adored their son. They were so often away on royal duties that they wanted to give him anything and everything he asked for so that he knew just how much they loved him. "No good will come of it!" said Percival's nanny. "He has far too much already. And still he's never happy!" But nobody listened to her.

"I'm bored. I need something new to play with," said Percival, chomping down another cupcake.

"It's not some*thing* new you need," said Nanny, "but some*one*. You need friends, not toys and cake."

"But there are no other children in the palace," he said, "and the children in the village are so different. Anyway, they don't know me. They have each other, they don't need me. I'm all alone."

"Nonsense! See the children making a den?" She pointed out of the window. "Such fun! Go and join them."

"No. I'll get my new clothes muddy. I'll ask someone to bring me a trampoline instead." Within minutes the trampoline arrived and Percival bounced and bounced — and then felt sick. "This is hopeless!" he wailed. And he sat on the trampoline and began to cry.

Then he found he couldn't stop crying, and the more the tears poured, the more lonely he felt. What use were toys and clothes when he needed someone to comfort him? He went to the playroom to find Nanny, but she was too busy tidying away his toys to even notice him.

He sat on the windowsill and cried some more. In fact, he cried so much that his playroom filled with tears. Soon the toys and plates of food were bobbing like ships on the sea, and Nanny was floating on the toy train, using a tennis racket as an oar. "Stop crying or we'll soon be drowned!" she said. But Percival just kept wailing. He wailed so loudly that he broke the glass in the window, and the tears whooshed out of the palace in a great, gushing river, taking the toys with it. "Help!" cried Percival. "My toys!" But the river swept him out the window, too. "Help!" he cried again. "I can't swim!" How could he? The King and Queen had been too busy with their duties to teach him.

The children of the village stopped in awe. Rushing past them were the most beautiful toys they'd ever seen. Then they heard Percival's shouts. "Quick!" said one. And as Percival tumbled past, they caught him by his collar and hoisted him out of the water. Percival sat beside their den, muddy and wet.

"Thank you!" he exclaimed, forgetting that his toys were floating away. "You saved me!"

"Of course!" said the children. "Why wouldn't we?"

"You don't know me. You have each other; you don't need me ..." said Percival. The children looked puzzled.

"The more the merrier!" said one. "We'd like to get to know you!" And for what felt like the first time in his life, Percival smiled a big smile. He picked up a stick and laid it on the den. "I'd like to get to know you, too," he said.

Possessions can never make us truly happy. A wise person knows that joy comes from sharing our lives with others, even when they seem different to us.

The Invisible Elephant

Take a deep, relaxing breath, snuggle down and listen carefully to this tale about an elephant who thought he was invisible. Do you think he was *really* invisible? Let's read the story and find out.

Eric the elephant was standing at the edge of the jungle when he saw a shooting star. "I'll make a wish," he said.

"If I were you, I'd wish to be invisible," said Tommy the tiger, who was camouflaged in the tall grass. "You're so big. Hunters can easily see you and catch you."

"What a wonderful idea," said Eric, and he wished: "Oh, shooting star, if you can hear, make me vanish and disappear." But he could still see his trunk when he looked down. "My wish hasn't come true," he sighed.

Just then, Tommy decided to play a trick. "Where are you? I can hear your voice, but I can't see you!" he cried.

"Really?" Eric chuckled. "I must be invisible after all!" And the next morning he stomped through the jungle, imagining himself as transparent as the air.

"Hello. Can you see me?" he asked everyone he met. Tommy had warned them all not to spoil his trick, so even though the monkeys could see Eric, they chuckled and said, "We can't see you. You're invisible." Then they swung away through the trees, laughing at how silly Eric had been.

Eric, though, was delighted with his magic disguise. "Can you see me?" he asked the parrots.

"See *who*?" they squawked. "There's nobody there!" Then they flew away, shrieking with laughter.

"Amazing! I'll be safe from any hunters," said Eric. Then he saw a little mouse. "Hello, down there. Can you see me?" Elsa the mouse scurried away – she knew Tommy would be furious if she spoiled his trick, but she didn't want to lie to Eric. And later that day, as she was nibbling a berry, Elsa spotted elephant hunters coming through the jungle, carrying a big net. "Quick!" she called to a passing parrot. "Fly fast! Warn Eric he's not invisible!"

"No way!" said the parrot. "I'm scared of Tommy."

"Swing quickly to Eric," she begged a monkey, but the monkey cried, "I can't do that, Tommy will be angry!"

"But the hunters will catch Eric!" Elsa squeaked as she ran through the undergrowth. Then she saw the big elephant standing in a clearing, the jungle creatures still chuckling in the branches

72

above. "Run, Eric! Hunters are coming!" she cried.

Eric smiled. "I'm safe! I'm invisible. Everyone says so."

Elsa scurried along his trunk and pulled up his enormous ear. "You're not invisible!" she said. "Tommy the tiger played a trick. Now run, before the hunters throw their net." Eric was confused, but hearing the panic in the little mouse's voice, he turned quickly and thundered away.

That night Elsa lay relaxing on Eric's shoulder, staring at the starry sky. "Thank you, little friend," Eric said to Elsa. "I was silly to believe I was actually invisible. And foolish to trust Tommy. If you hadn't been brave enough to tell the truth, the hunters would have caught me."

"It's Tommy who needs to be brave now!" said Elsa, spotting the tiger's shadow in the long grass. "He should be brave enough to come out and apologise."

"Quite right!" chorused the parrots and the monkeys from their resting places in the treetops.

"Alright! Alright! I'm sorry!" mumbled Tommy. And he slunk off, wishing that *he* could disappear ...

It takes courage to tell the truth when others won't speak up. A wise person knows that true friends treat each other with compassion and honesty.

The Teddy
Bear Tussle

Take a deep, relaxing breath, snuggle down and listen carefully to this tale about a girl called Polly who loved her teddy bear Bruno. What do you think happened to Bruno? Let's read the story and find out.

Polly had been given Bruno when she was a baby. Everywhere Polly went, the teddy bear went too – except, that is, to school. "Bringing toys to school is not allowed," said Polly's teacher, Mrs Robinson. But at times Polly couldn't bear to be parted from Bruno. One day, she crammed him into the pocket of her hoody, before setting off for school. Bruno stayed hidden all through morning lessons. But at lunchtime, as Polly walked across the playground, a boy called Luke noticed Bruno's furry ear.

"What's that?" he shouted. Before Polly could answer, he yanked Bruno out of his hiding place.

"Ha!" he roared. "I've got your ted!"

"Be careful!" Polly cried, as Luke ran round the playground, swinging poor Bruno by his ear. "Stop!"

75

begged Polly. But Luke wouldn't listen. He wanted to keep the smartly dressed bear for himself.

Luke ran round the playground quicker than ever, but Polly was even faster. "Got you!" she yelled, grabbing Bruno by the leg. "Now let him go."

"I won't!" said Luke, tugging at Bruno's arm. "He's mine now!" he goaded.

"No!" gasped Polly. "Give him back!" But Luke only pulled harder. Polly tugged too. "Let go!" she screamed.

"No!" roared Luke.

They yanked and pulled, stretching poor Bruno between them. Then suddenly Polly heard a horrible tearing sound. Bruno's arm was coming away from his body! Luke kept pulling, but Polly let go. She loved the teddy far too much to allow him to be torn in two.

"Alright!" she cried. "You have him then!" And she burst into tears.

Luke ran off, whooping for joy. "I've got your teddy! I've got your ted!" he sang unkindly.

Hearing the commotion, Mrs Robinson came outside. "What's going on?" she asked. Polly wanted to explain that Luke had taken her beloved teddy but she didn't dare say anything. She knew toys weren't allowed at school.

"What's the matter, dear?" said Mrs Robinson, gently. "Don't cry. Tell me what happened."

"I brought my teddy to school," sobbed Polly to her teacher. "I'm sorry." Luke stopped running and stared guiltily at Bruno's torn arm.

Mrs Robinson took the little bear from him and examined the damage to his arm as Polly told her how she and Luke had fought over Bruno.

"You were very brave, Polly. Letting go of something you love so much must have been a hard thing to do," she said. "And it's a good job you did let go – otherwise his arm would have come off altogether. As it is, with a few careful stitches, I think he'll be as good as new."

"Thank goodness!" cried Polly, gently taking Bruno from her teacher and giving him a big hug.

"Take him home to be mended tonight and don't bring him back to school again," said Mrs Robinson firmly.

Mrs Robinson turned to Luke, who was staring at his shoes. "As for you, young man, you know very well it is wrong to take things that belong to other people …" But Polly didn't hear any more. She was busy tucking Bruno away – very safely – until hometime.

Sometimes we need to be brave and let go of something – or someone – we love. A wise person knows there are different ways of being courageous.

The Singing Canary

Take a deep, relaxing breath, snuggle down and listen carefully to this tale about a happy sparrow called Mack who, one day, became very envious and unhappy. What do you think happened to make him feel like that? Let's read the story and find out.

It was a warm spring morning. Tired from swooping through the sky, Mack flapped his feathers and settled to rest on the branch of a tree. He could see for miles over the sunlit fields. What a wonderful view!

Mack opened his beak and sang. "Oh, what a beautiful morning!" His chirp crackled in the still air. "Oh, what a beautiful day!"

Then suddenly he heard another voice – a birdsong so sweet it made his feathers tremble: "Oh, what a beautiful morning …" The tune was the same, but it sounded so pure, so fresh, so much finer than his own sharp voice.

Behind a hedge was a little, white farmhouse. "That must be where the singing is coming from," he chirped.

He fluttered over to land on the windowsill. And then he froze. He had expected to see another dusty sparrow like him, or maybe a slate-grey starling. Perhaps even a robin with a fine red breast. But the bird Mack saw was far more handsome than that. He had wonderful yellow feathers as bright as the sun.

"Who are you? *What* are you?" Mack gasped. The little yellow bird stopped singing and turned his head. "I'm a canary," said the bird, and his sweet voice rippled with warm laughter. "My name is Apollo."

"Apollo? Ha! What a silly name." Mack was surprised by his own harsh words, but he didn't take them back. He wanted to tease the bird with the fancy name, fine feathers and beautiful voice. "I heard you showing off with your singing," he snapped. "You interrupted my song."

"I didn't mean to show off," said Apollo. "I'm sorry. The sunlight on the garden looked so lovely that it made me want to sing …" Apollo trailed off and looked so sad that Mack felt ashamed.

"It's not fair," Mack sighed. "I've always liked my brown feathers, but looking at you, I realize how scruffy I am. And I love to sing, but compared to yours, my song is as tuneless as a frog's croak." He shuffled awkwardly on the sill. "I'm jealous," he admitted.

80

"*You?* Jealous of *me?*" Apollo shook his head. "Don't be jealous of me, my friend. My feathers and my voice are nothing. Rather, I should be jealous of you!"

Mack gave a rattly chirp of disbelief and looked at his brown wings. "What do I have that you could ever want?"

"You have the greatest gift of all," said Apollo. "You have freedom." The canary spread his golden wings and lifted from his perch – but he flapped only twice and then fell back. Something was holding him back.

"Oh my! You're tied down," gasped Mack, noticing a thin silver chain fastened around Apollo's leg. The other end was attached securely to the perch.

"I can never fly away," Apollo said. "I will never feel the breeze on my feathers. I will never sing in the blue sky."

"That's terrible!" said Mack. He was only an ordinary sparrow, but he was as free as the wind. "I'm sorry," he said. "Let's be friends. When I visit, we can sing together." Apollo agreed, and they began to sing their song: "Oh, what a beautiful morning …"

Envy can blind us to the suffering of others. A wise person appreciates what they have in their own life instead of wanting to be like other people.

The Princess and the Precious Pearls

Take a deep, relaxing breath, snuggle down and listen carefully to this tale about a princess called Aster, who lost something very special. What do you think happened? Let's read the story and find out.

One hot afternoon, Princess Aster put on her swimsuit and hurried across the palace gardens toward the cool bathing pools beneath the shady trees. Overhead, the palace monkeys dozed quietly in the branches.

"Good to see you're behaving yourselves," Princess Aster called out, remembering how just last week the monkeys had played frisbee with her mother's crown. At the edge of a large pool, she kicked off her sandals and was about to leap in when she remembered that she was wearing her string of precious rose-coloured pearls.

"Argh!" she said. "I should have left the necklace in my bedroom." The priceless pearls had belonged Princess Aster's great-great-grandmother. She did not dare wear them while she was swimming.

83

Princess Aster knew she should run back to the palace and put the pearls safely in her jewellery box, but it was so hot. "It will take too long!" she said. She glanced across the long lawns and saw Oliver, the baker's boy from the village, huffing and puffing with a huge hamper of bread and cakes for the palace. She gave him a friendly wave. "It's nearly time for tea," Aster sighed. "If I go back now there won't be time to swim!" She hid the pearls under her towel at the foot of a tree. "The necklace will be safe there," she told herself. Then she dived into the cool water with a splash. "Yippee!"

Unknown to Aster, not all the monkeys were asleep. Peeping down through the branches, a golden-coloured monkey called Moss had seen her take off the shiny pearls, then dive into the water. "Oooh! I do love things that sparkle," she cooed. Quick as a flash, she leapt down, grabbed the necklace, then swung away through the branches before anyone could see what she had done – least of all Princess Aster, who was still happily splashing.

Ten minutes later, Aster's tutor called her in for tea. Aster climbed out of the pool, picked up her towel – and froze in horror. "Help!" she wailed, "My pearls are gone!"

The palace guards ran from all corners of the garden, crashing through the trees. "Who has stolen the pearls?" they cried. "Someone must have seen who took them!"

Then they spied Oliver returning down the drive, having made his delivery, the now-empty hamper on his back. "Stop!" cried the guards, charging after Oliver. He took fright at their angry voices and, without thinking, dropped the hamper, turned on his heels and ran. The monkeys squawked in the trees.

"Quick! The boy is running away!" panted the Captain of the Guards, charging after him. "It must be him!"

Oliver tried to scramble over the palace gates, but he was too slow. "Got you!" said the captain, grabbing the poor boy by the ankle and pulling him to the ground.

"I haven't done anything wrong!" cried Oliver.

"Fibber!" barked the captain. "You are the only stranger inside the palace grounds. It *must* have been you who stole the necklace."

The guards searched Oliver and the hamper but found nothing. "Where have you hidden it?" demanded the captain, furiously. He marched Oliver off to see the King.

Oliver sunk down to his knees before the throne. "It wasn't me who took the necklace, Your Majesty," he tried to explain. But the King was too angry to listen.

"If you are not the thief, why did you try to run away?" he bellowed. Without waiting for an answer, he ordered Oliver to be locked up until he told them what he had done with the necklace. "Please believe me!" begged

Oliver, as he was led away. "I'm innocent."

"Oh, this is not right," said Princess Aster to her tutor when she heard what had happened. "Oliver and I are friends — we often talk when he drops off a delivery. I know he wouldn't take my necklace."

"Well, I agree with His Majesty. If the boy didn't take it, why did he try to run away?" her tutor asked.

"I don't know," said Princess Aster. It was true, running away did make Oliver look guilty, but they had waved to each other before her swim — why would he take her pearls? She tried to think calmly.

"I expect Oliver was scared because the guards were chasing him," she said at last. "I would have run away too. Even the monkeys were frightened." She glanced out of the window and saw the monkeys in the trees by the pool — no longer sleeping, but chattering loudly to one another.

"Of course!" she gasped. "The mischievous monkeys! I bet it was one of them!" Aster dashed upstairs to her bedroom and grabbed a toy tiara and a handful of sparkly sequins from her dressing-up box. She marched back down the stairs. "Follow me," she said to the grown-ups. "I think I know who the real thief is!"

Aster ran to the edge of the pool, laid the toy jewels at the foot of the tree and then crept away to hide. "Shh!" she said, putting her finger to her lips. The King, the guards and her tutor hid, too. It was only a moment before naughty little Moss the monkey appeared.

"Oooh, look!" she chattered to herself. "More sparkly jewels." She swung down from the trees, a string of pretty pearls dangling round her neck.

"Stop! Thief!" The captain grabbed the cheeky monkey by the tail.

"Careful!" cried Princess Aster. "She's only a playful little monkey. She didn't know how precious the jewels were." She gently unclipped the necklace from Moss's neck. "I'm afraid you can't keep my pearls," Princess Aster explained. "But you can have my toy tiara, if you like."

"Oooh!" The little monkey swung away, delighted with her shiny prize. And Princess Aster fastened the precious necklace safely around her own neck. "We owe Oliver an apology," she said.

"I am proud of you, Aster," said the King. "I should have stopped to think before jumping to the wrong conclusion."

"And I should have been more careful with my jewels!" said Princess Aster. "We have all learned a lesson today."

Try not to jump to conclusions or react hastily when you're angry. A wise person stays calm and gathers all the evidence, taking time to find out the truth.

The Chameleon
and the Crickets

Take a deep, relaxing breath, snuggle down and listen carefully to this tale about a chameleon who boasted that she could catch seven juicy crickets. Do you think she succeeded? Let's read the story and find out.

There was once an old chameleon called Maya who could change to any colour. "I can even make myself the same colour as you!" she boasted to her friend Sienna, the orange tree frog. And, just like that, she turned bright amber, like a traffic light.

"When I'm camouflaged, I'm invisible," Maya said, turning emerald-green and hiding herself in the leaves. "Insects crawl past and …" BAM! She stuck out her long, sticky tongue and grabbed a passing beetle.

"That's good," croaked Sienna. "But anyone can catch a beetle." And she stuck out her own tongue and caught a beetle, too. "Even with your trick of changing colour," said Sienna, "I bet you don't catch many crickets. They can leap as high as the sky."

"I can catch a juicy cricket any time I like," said Maya. "Crickets are my favourite food."

"Good!" said Sienna. "I shall come to dinner at yours next Saturday. That gives you seven days to catch seven fat crickets for our feast – one cricket every day."

"Simple," boasted Maya. But she knew Sienna was right – catching crickets wasn't easy. On the first day, Maya turned green and hid among the leaves. Soon, a band of singing crickets came by. "Ha!" thought Maya. "I'm invisible." BAM! Out went her tongue.

"Look out!" cried Captain Cricket, and all the crickets leapt safely into the air, out of the chameleon's reach.

On the second day, Maya turned brown and hid among the twigs. But it was just the same. "Look out!" cried Captain Cricket. And off bounced the crickets across the meadow, singing their merry song.

On the third day, the chameleon turned yellow and hid among the dry grass. "Look out!" cried Captain Cricket.

"Three days have gone by," sighed Maya, as the band bounced away. "Sienna will never let me forget it if I don't have seven fat crickets on a plate on Saturday."

So, on the fourth day, the chameleon tried something new. Instead of hiding, she turned blue and lay on top of a hollow log by the river where the crickets could easily see her. "What's the matter?" said Captain Cricket as he came past. "Aren't you going to hide and try to eat us?"

"No!" Maya hung her tongue out of the corner of her mouth. "I'm too old and tired. My hunting days are over. I'll just lie here and rest."

"Oh, dear!" said the kind captain. "Let us bring you some water." And he called to his band of crickets. "Follow me to the river. We will each bring back a drop of water on our wings for poor old Maya."

"Yes, sir!" agreed the crickets and they all hopped toward the river, singing their song.

But … BAM! Just as the last cricket was passing by, Maya threw out her tongue like a whip and caught the little insect by the leg. "Got you!" She stuffed the cricket inside the log and blocked up the end with a rock. "Just six more of your friends," she whispered, "and I will have a juicy feast to share with Sienna."

Meanwhile, at the front of the troop, Captain Cricket hadn't noticed anything amiss and he carried on to the river. The crickets collected water and brought it back for the chameleon. Later that night, as they were settling down to sleep, the crickets finally noticed that one of their band was missing. The next day, they were too sad to sing.

"What's the matter?" asked Maya, still pretending to be exhausted as she lay on the bank.

"We've lost one of our comrades," said the captain. "We'll bring you water while we search for him."

And off they all went toward the river. BAM! Maya's strong, sticky tongue shot out and she caught another cricket from the end of the line. That evening the band were distraught to find they'd lost yet another friend.

"What is happening to us?" the remaining crickets asked the captain.

"I don't know," he said. Then, the next day, yet another cricket disappeared. "The one who vanishes is always at the back of the line," said the captain. "I can't see what's happening because I'm at the front." He rubbed his feet together and thought long and hard.

"Perhaps I was wrong to trust Maya," he said at last. "Perhaps she has not given up hunting at all. Tomorrow, I'll walk at the back of the line and see what happens."

So, the next morning, the crickets set out with the captain at the back. "Here they come!" chuckled Maya. BAM! Out shot her tongue as the last cricket in line hopped by.

But the captain was ready for the devious chameleon. He

leapt into the air, safely out of the way. "What have you done with the other crickets?" demanded the captain, landing on a leaf.

"I gobbled them up," lied Maya. But as she spoke, her eyes darted toward the end of the log.

"No, you didn't!" shouted the captain, realizing the missing crickets were trapped inside the log. He clapped his legs together and all the crickets began to dance in circles round and round Maya.

"Stop! You're making me dizzy!" she cried.

But they just spun faster and faster, distracting Maya while the captain used a stick to lever the stone away from the log, freeing the crickets inside. "We may be small," he said to Maya, "but we are clever! We worked out your trick and now you have nothing to eat!" Then the whole band bounced away, singing happily once again.

And so Maya had no crickets to offer Sienna. "Not quite the hunter you thought you were?" laughed her friend when she arrived. She thought it was so funny, she didn't mind that there was nothing at all for supper.

Our brains are the greatest strength we have. A wise person uses their intelligence to solve problems and help others, not to play tricks or cheat.

Betty's
Big Day

Take a deep, relaxing breath, snuggle down and listen carefully to this tale about an adventurous hen named Betty Doodle-Doo. She longed to join the circus, but she very nearly lost her chance. What do you think can have happened? Let's read the story and find out.

Betty Doodle-Doo flapped her wings with excitement. A travelling circus had pitched its tent in the field behind the farm. She flew up to balance on top of a rope that she'd strung like a high-wire between two trees.

"Wow!" cheeped her little brother and two little sisters, the triplet chicks. "You're an acrobat, Betty!"

Betty clucked and bowed her head. "You know it's my dream to join the circus," she said.

Across the fence, at the neighbouring farm, someone else was watching Betty. Toffi Rooster was from a grand and wealthy family of chickens. He had fallen in love with Betty from afar. "What a beautiful young hen," he thought, and he strutted across the field to talk to her.

"Come and see the circus with me tonight," he said. "I will buy a pot of golden corn for us to share at the show. Two pots if you wish. I will give you anything!"

"Wow!" Betty was taken aback. She had planned to take the triplets to the circus that night. "I can't ..." she began.

But Betty's mother and father had seen Toffi Rooster admiring her and they thought he would be a very good husband for their daughter.

"Of course you should go to the circus with Toffi tonight," said Betty's father. "We can take the chicks to see the show tomorrow."

So Betty and Toffi went to the circus.

Toffi had arranged the best perch in the middle of the front row, with seeds, nuts and corn for them to share.

The show began. Betty stared in amazement with her beak open wide. "Aren't they magnificent?" she said as the acrobats tumbled and turned. "If only I could be up there with them."

Then the funny duck clowns came on and she laughed until she cried.

"Thank you for taking me, Toffi," she said when the show was over. "I had a wonderful time."

But Toffi had hardly noticed what was happening in the big top. He had eyes only for Betty. As he dropped her back at her hen house, he said, "You're so beautiful. I'll tell your parents I want to marry you!" And at the top of his voice he crowed: "I want to be with you for ever!"

Before Betty could say a word, everyone had heard his calls and there was much clucking and crowing with excitement. "Such a rich and handsome groom," said her mother. "What a magnificent wedding we'll have."

Betty thought of her dream to join the circus. Perhaps being the centre of attention at her own wedding would be just as much fun as performing for the crowd in the big top. "Well, maybe …" she said.

"I must go," said Toffi. "I must tell my parents the plan." And he strutted away across the fields. "See you at dawn the day after tomorrow," he called back to her. "We shall be married in the light of the rising sun."

Betty's family could talk of nothing but the Roosters' magnificent home: the feed shed full of grain and the nesting boxes stuffed with the softest hay. Betty imagined the fine life she would have at the fancy farm.

Toffi's family were also delighted to hear the news. But they were very superstitious, too. They wanted to be sure the marriage would bring good fortune for their son. "You must wear this garland of berries for good luck," clucked his mother, placing the garland around his neck.

However, the next day the Rooster family's trusted advisor Sniffles Baloney, the turkey, shook his head. "That garland will do no good," he said. Usually, they consulted him about *everything*. But Toffi had got carried away. He had made an important decision all by himself – and Sniffles wasn't having that. "No. No. No!" he scolded. "You can't get married at dawn the day after tomorrow. It would be most unlucky. You need to wait."

Toffi was crestfallen, but he agreed. With a heavy heart, he retreated to his coop. However, nobody thought to tell Betty that the wedding had been postponed.

So, as the sun rose the next morning, Betty stood wearing a wedding dress, waiting for her groom. For the first time since Toffi's proposal, Betty had time to think about what she really wanted. "I don't want to get married! I want to join the circus," she said. But no one was listening.

"He will be here soon," clucked her mother, glancing across the empty fields. "He'd better be," chirped her father. "I have filled three troughs with corn for the wedding feast." But by the time the sun was high in the sky, there was still no sign of Toffi. "This is boring!" tweeted the chicks. "We can't wait any longer."

"No, we can't!" said Betty. Two fields away an excited

crowd was gathering outside the big top as the circus performers got ready for their next show. All Betty wanted was to join them.

"I know you want the best for me," she said to her family, "but this wedding plan has made me realize all the more that I *have* to follow my dream!" She hugged and kissed her parents goodbye. "How lucky that Toffi didn't come! Please come and watch me very soon," she said, as she set off toward the big top.

Meanwhile, on the Roosters' farm, Sniffles Baloney had finally decided the time was right. "This is it," he told Toffi. "This is the perfect time for a lucky wedding." Toffi straightened his feathers and hopped out of his coop. He ran across the fields. But when he arrived at Betty's farm, the little chicks sighed and said, "You're too late!"

"She's gone?" asked Toffi in disbelief. The chicks and Mr and Mrs Doodle-Doo nodded. Toffi looked across at the circus. "I wish I hadn't listened to Sniffles. I should have been brave enough to follow my own heart," he said. "But I am glad that Betty was able to follow hers."

It takes patience and reflection to know your own mind. A wise person is not swayed by the ambitions others have for them – or by the idea of "bad luck".

Uncle Onion's Garden

Take a deep, relaxing breath, snuggle down and listen carefully to this tale about a wise old gardener called Uncle Onion. One day, he left his garden in the care of his young nephew. What do you think happened to the plants and flowers? Let's read the story and find out.

Uncle Onion was singing loudly to his tomatoes when there was an almighty clatter from his potting shed. He stopped singing, hobbled over and threw open the door. Basil, his nephew, was surrounded by broken flower pots.

"Whatever is going on?" harumphed Uncle Onion.

"A huge mosquito bit me. I tried to hit it with the spade," cried Basil. "I didn't mean to smash the pots. The mosquito just wouldn't stay still!" The tiny mosquito pirouetted in the corner of the shed, took a bow and buzzed off past Uncle Onion. "It's getting away!" shouted Basil, wildly swinging the spade, nearly hitting his uncle on the head.

"Never mind the mosquito! Look at the terrible mess you've made!" roared Uncle Onion in a deep, angry voice.

I'm sorry, Uncle Onion," said Basil. "I promise I'll make it up to you."

"If you really want to make it up to me, you can start by clearing up this mess," scowled Uncle Onion. "I have to go to the market to buy some seeds. When I get back I want to see this shed spick and span and every plant in the garden watered. Can you do that?"

Basil was too embarrassed to admit that he had never watered a garden before. "Of course!" he said.

Uncle Onion's garden had lots of different plants. Basil gulped. He had no idea how much water he needed for each one. "I'll ask my friends, the beavers. They're so clever," he thought. Basil whistled loudly. In no time at all, three mischievous young beavers – Teeny, Tiny and Toty – rolled through the garden gate, giggling and tickling each other. When Basil told them about chasing the mosquito with his spade, they fell about with laughter.

"But things are serious now," said Basil. "Uncle Onion is very cross. I want to prove to him how responsible I can be. But I've no idea how to water the garden properly."

"No problem!" said Toty in his best grown-up voice. "We'll be able to help!" Teeny and Tiny nodded.

"Awesome!" cried Basil. "The water is in those big barrels over there, and the watering cans are next to them. I think we just have to dunk a watering can in a

barrel to fill it with water, then wave it above the plants like rain. I saw Uncle Onion do it once."

"That's right!" said Toty wisely. "Now you go and clear up the mess in the shed and we'll sort out the watering."

"Thank you," said Basil, and he hurried off, trusting that the beavers would know what to do.

At first, the beavers managed only to soak themselves, which they found hilarious. But, after several tries with a watering can, they started to get the hang of it.

"How do we know if we've used enough water?" asked Teeny.

"No idea," said Tiny. "We could ask Basil."

"Don't be silly!" said Toty. "Basil doesn't know! That's why he asked us in the first place. We're the clever ones!"

"Good point. I know! Let's pull the plants up and see if the roots are wet," suggested Teeny.

"Brilliant!" cried Toty. And, with great enthusiasm, the beavers methodically watered each plant, then pulled it out of the ground to check that the roots were wet.

"This watering can is too small!" exclaimed Teeny after several minutes. "I can't be bothered to keep refilling it and then pulling up every plant."

"Time for a rest!" said Tiny, throwing himself on the ground, pretending to faint from exhaustion.

"Exactly!" agreed Teeny falling onto Tiny.

"Pile on! Mud bath!" called Toty, throwing himself on top of the others. The beavers rolled around in the wet soil, covering themselves in mud and giggling wildly.

"I've had a brilliant idea," said Teeny. "Rather than filling the watering can, why don't we just take the lid off one of the barrels and roll it down the garden? The water will spray out and the whole garden will be watered!"

"Awesome!" agreed the other two. The beavers took the lid off the biggest barrel and, with lots of huffing and puffing, pushed it over onto its side.

Water gushed out and the barrel started rolling down the garden. "Look out!" cried Teeny. The little beavers scampered through the mud, diving out of the barrel's path. "Oh no!" shouted Toty as the barrel gathered speed, crushing several rows of flowers. "Yikes!" yelled Tiny as the barrel headed for the veg patch. It was only at this point that Basil heard the beavers' shrieks and yelps. He rushed outside, just in time to see the barrel explode against the wall – and Teeny, Tiny and Toty collapse into giggles.

"What have you *done*?" Basil gasped. Before the beavers could answer, they heard a deep roar from the garden gate. "What on earth is going on?"

"Yikes! It's Uncle Onion! Run for it!" cried Teeny. And without so much as a sorry, the little beavers were gone.

"Basil!" thundered Uncle Onion. "My garden …"

"I asked my friends the beavers for help," quivered Basil. "I didn't know what to do and I thought they did."

"Beavers?! Why didn't you ask *me*?" sighed Uncle Onion, his voice softening. Basil shrugged his shoulders and sniffed. "Come on, now. There's no point crying over sticky mud. What's done is done. And I'll teach you how we can sort it all out." He handed Basil the spade. "Start by digging holes for the plants that have been ripped up … And get those beavers back. We'll need help to get this done."

"Yes, Uncle," said Basil, and he whistled for the beavers.

Everyone worked hard – even Teeny, Tiny and Toty. "Where should I put this plant?" asked Toty, suddenly keen to learn from the wise, old uncle.

"Over there, in that big hole Teeny and Tiny have dug," said Uncle Onion. Then he looked at the little beavers and his nephew all working so hard and smiled. "You know what?" he said, putting his arm round Basil's shoulders. "I might just make gardeners out of you yet."

Be brave enough to ask for advice from someone who has more experience than you. A wise person is always ready to learn from a good teacher.

The Golden Shell

Take a deep, relaxing breath, snuggle down and listen carefully to this tale about a mermaid called Marina who wore a beautiful golden shell pendant around her neck. One day, she lent it to the Octopus Queen. What do you think happened? Let's read the story and find out.

Marina was a wonderful singer who travelled the oceans performing her enchanting songs. Once, she came to the underwater palace of the Octopus Queen.

"Shall I sing for Your Majesty?" she asked.

"Oh yes!" cried the Octopus Queen. She had heard of Marina's fame and couldn't wait to hear the young mermaid sing. But, as soon as Marina stepped on stage, it was not only her voice that captivated the Queen – it was also the huge, shimmering gold shell she wore. As Marina sang, the golden necklace glistened and the Queen was entranced.

"What a beautiful shell," she said to the young mermaid when her performance was over.

"Thank you," said Marina. "My father gave it to me. It's the most precious thing I own."

"It's fabulous," said the Queen. "I wish I could wear it tonight. I'm giving a royal dinner. I'd be the envy of every underwater king and queen with that golden shell around my neck."

"Then you must wear it to your dinner," said Marina kindly. "As long as I can have it back tomorrow."

Delighted by Marina's generosity, the Queen promised, "I will return it first thing tomorrow morning."

Marina unhooked the shell and gave it to the Queen, who attached it to a necklace of her own and fastened it around her neck.

The Queen was indeed the envy of all who saw her.

"A gorgeous necklace," gasped the Queen of Crabs.

"A rare jewel indeed," agreed the Empress of Sharks.

That night, once the guests had gone, the Octopus Queen sighed. "I wish I could keep the shell," she said. Then a dreadful idea came to her. "Why *shouldn't* I keep it? I am the Queen, after all. I can have whatever I want."

Next morning, Marina arrived to take back her shell. "I hope you enjoyed the party, Your Highness. May I have my pendant back now?" she asked.

"Oh dear!" The Octopus Queen tried her best to look sad. "I'm afraid I can't give it back."

"Why?" stammered Marina. "What's happened?"

"Erm …" The Queen glanced around her coral palace, trying desperately to think of an excuse. "Er … your necklace has vanished," she said unconvincingly.

"Vanished?" Marina felt a ripple of fear. "How?"

"Er … it was eaten by a fish!" said the Queen.

"A fish?" A tear rolled down Marina's cheek. She knew the Queen was lying, but she wasn't brave enough to challenge her. And anyway, before she could say another word, the Queen turned away. "I'm sorry I can't return your trinket," she said and fled to her royal chamber.

"Oh, Marina!" said an angel fish swimming nearby. "Don't cry. How could a fish have eaten that big shell?"

"Oh, I know," Marina sighed. "But the Queen is never going to give it back! She has kept it for herself."

"What a thief!" gasped a passing clownfish.

"What a scoundrel!" agreed a blue tang, appearing from behind a piece of coral.

"Steal something of hers!" said the angel fish. "She has whole caves full of jewels. Get your revenge!"

The other fish agreed, but Marina shook her head. "No," she said. "I'll wait. I'm sure the Queen will do the right thing. A stolen necklace can bring her no pleasure."

In her chamber the Queen had slipped the golden shell around her neck again. But Marina was right. As the

Queen admired the jewel, she sighed. She knew she could never leave her chamber wearing the necklace. If she did, everyone would know her story about the fish had been a lie, and she would become known as a common thief.

From beneath the window, in the coral reef below, the Queen heard Marina's soft, sweet voice. The song she sang was beautiful but very sad – a lament for her lost golden shell, a precious gift from her father.

Feeling guilty, the Queen slammed shut her box of jewels. "I can't wear the necklace to Marina's concert tonight … And the mermaid sounds so sad."

She knew what she had to do.

"Marina!" she called, as she hurried out of her chamber and into the coral reef below, "It's very strange but I think the fish who swallowed your necklace must have spat it out again. Look what I found!" And she held out the shimmering pendant.

"What a fibber!" muttered the blue tang.

"She's still not telling the truth," sighed the clownfish.

"She's a royal disgrace!" grumbled the angel fish.

But Marina just smiled.

"Oh! How clever of you to find my lost necklace, Your Majesty!" she cried. "Thank you for giving it back."

"You're welcome!" said the Queen. But being face to face with Marina reminded her of how kind Marina had

been to lend her the necklace in the first place. Blushing and squirming, the Queen couldn't keep up her lie. "I'm sorry," she whispered. "I did something terrible."

Marina put her finger to the Queen's lips. "I have the pendant. That's all that matters," she said. Then she smiled brighter than the golden jewel itself. "Why don't you wear it to my concert tonight? Keep the necklace safe for me while I perform."

"Really?" the Queen gasped. "You'd trust me?"

"Of course," said Marina. "I know this time you'll give it back to me."

"As long as there aren't any more hungry fish about!" muttered the clownfish. The blue tang and the angel fish giggled cheekily among the coral.

But Marina and the Queen didn't hear. The mermaid was already swimming off to get ready for the concert and the Octopus Queen had hurried off to find the perfect tiara to match the golden shell … even though she knew it would be hers for only one more night.

Dishonesty of any kind tends to lead to unhappiness. A wise person knows that honesty in both our words and deeds is what makes us truly happy.

Tintoretto, the Mouse from Town

Take a deep, relaxing breath, snuggle down and listen carefully to this tale about Colin, a country mouse who made friends with a town mouse. What do you think happened to them? Let's read the story and find out.

After a year in the big city, Colin, the country mouse, was coming home. He'd loved the noise and bustle for a while, but now he longed to return to his peaceful home at the edge of a cornfield. His friend Tintoretto, a shabby, grey town mouse, was coming home with him.

"Almost there now," he told Tintoretto. In excitement, Tintoretto twitched his ragged ear (the result of a narrow escape from an alley cat) and swished his stubby tail (a cart had run over it). That his friend looked rough and ragged didn't matter to Colin. Tintoretto was kind and brave – just last week Tintoretto had saved Colin from nearly drowning in a city drain.

"Tintoretto," he grinned, "I can't wait to show you the cornfield and introduce you to my friends and family."

"I can't wait to meet them!" said Tintoretto. "I know how much you've missed them while you've been away."

As the pair reached the edge of the cornfield, little mice began to appear, twitching their whiskers and squeaking with excitement when they saw Colin on the path. "Welcome home!" they cried.

"Hello!" Colin scampered forward. "Meet my friend, Tintoretto. He's come with me from the city."

"Tintoretto? What a strange name," tittered Colin's cousin Carol. And all her brothers and sisters began to giggle under their breath, too.

"Look at his ragged ear," whispered one.

"And look at his tail," squeaked another. "It's so short."

"And his dull fur. He's almost like a rat!" squealed a third.

Colin knew that his friend had heard every word. "Don't worry," he explained. "My cousins aren't used to strangers. They've never been beyond this cornfield. As soon as they get to know you, they'll treat you as a friend."

"If they're as kind as you, I'm sure they will," Tintoretto replied, smiling.

That night there was a great celebration to welcome Colin home. The country mice brought corn from the field, berries from the hedgerows and acorns from the wood. Everyone wanted to hear of Colin's adventures.

"Tell us about the markets!" cried Cousin Charlie.

"Yes! Were there cheese stalls?" asked Cousin Carol.

"What about the alley cats?" shuddered Cousin Chester.

"Well …" As Colin began to answer, he glanced down the long, wooden table and saw that his friend was staring into space, looking lost and alone. "I was only a visitor to the big city," he said. "If you really want to know what it's like, you should ask Tintoretto. He's lived there all his life."

No one moved. "Why are none of you speaking to Tintoretto?" whispered Colin. "Why aren't you making him feel welcome?"

"I don't want to talk to a shabby town mouse," said Carol. "I don't like the way he looks."

"He smells strange. Like oil and gas and the city streets," said Charlie.

"I don't understand his strange accent," said Chester.

Colin stood up. "I'm ashamed of you all," he said. "Tintoretto's family made me welcome, but you've decided he's different and you're not trying to be kind." He stood up and went to sit with Tintoretto. The two friends shared a pile of ripe corn.

As the sun set over the fields, the mice began to dance and sing. It was a great party, but still no one spoke to Tintoretto. Instead, they nudged each other and whispered as he walked past. Colin tried to include his friend, but his family and schoolfriends surrounded him,

bombarding him with questions about the city. At last Tintoretto tapped Colin on the shoulder.

"I think I'll head back to town," he said. "I've forgotten some business I should attend to." Of course, this wasn't true, but Tintoretto didn't want to stay where he wasn't welcome.

"Don't go," pleaded Colin. "I thought you were going to stay for a month and be my guest."

"I'm sorry," sighed Tintoretto. "I can't."

"Good riddance!" whispered someone.

Colin spun around, but he didn't catch who had spoken.

"Yes! Go back to town, stranger," hissed someone else.

Colin was deeply disappointed by his friends and family. "Please stay the night," he begged.

Tintoretto shook his head. "It's best I'm on my way."

"At least let me walk you to the lane," said Colin.

"No need. Stay and enjoy your party. You are the guest of honour," said Tintoretto. "There's a full moon giving plenty of light. I can easily find my way."

Colin watched as Tintoretto set off toward the lane. His heart was heavy without his friend – there was no joy left in the celebrations. He turned to go.

Suddenly, there was a cry from the edge of the cornfield. It was Tintoretto! "Hide!" he shouted. "I've seen an owl!" The shabby town mouse ran bravely toward the country mice, making sure everyone could hear him. "An owl is coming. Hide!"

Quick as a flash, the little mice ran for cover in trees and bushes. The great bird swooped over, looking hungrily for prey. Tintoretto and Colin crouched in a hollow log. Carol and Charlie wriggled in next to them. "Thank you!" Carol said, squeezing Tintoretto's paw, once the owl had flown on by.

"You saved our lives," agreed Charlie.

"It's nothing," said Tintoretto.

"It's everything," said Colin. "You're a true friend."

Carol felt very bad. "We're sorry we didn't talk to you earlier. We'd all like to be your friends now – if you'll have us," she said.

"We were rude," agreed Charlie. "Please forgive us."

Tintoretto smiled. "Of course I forgive you. Any friend of Colin's is a friend of mine," he said. And, as all the country mice gradually came out of hiding, they gathered around the town mouse to hear his stories – and dance together until dawn.

Appearances don't count for anything – it's the goodness in someone's heart that matters. A wise person looks below the surface to find a friend.

Learning to Meditate

The three guided meditations in the pages that follow can be used to settle your child down before storytime, to help them get off to sleep after the story, or, at any time of day, to support the development of a more "mindful" way of living (see pages 18–19 for more on mindfulness). Each of them will, in different ways, help your child explore the connection between their mind and their body, and come to have a better understanding of how their thoughts, feelings and actions influence one another.

There are many different meditation techniques. Below are some easy-to-follow guidelines on how to approach practising meditation with your child.

Finding the right time and place

With any new skill we want to develop, repetition is the key. Try to practise meditation with your child at the same time each day and in the same place. The regularity and quality of the meditation are more important than the length of time you spend doing it. Stopping for even 5 minutes a day to rest and take the mind away from day-to-day concerns often has calming effects that ripple on far longer than you might expect. And the more often you practise, the farther the ripples will spread.

If possible, find somewhere to practise where both you and your child feel warm, comfortable and safe – somewhere that is quiet and where you will not be disturbed. When reading the meditations to your child, take your time and allow for pauses so that they have time to really imagine and experience the scenes that you are describing. It is the mind's nature to wander, so don't worry if your child becomes distracted at times when doing a visualization. It's completely normal. Simply remind them that all they have to do is gently and kindly bring their attention back to the sensations in their body, and continue with the meditation.

Getting comfortable

Avoid restrictive clothing that distracts from the meditation. Your child is likely to be in their nightclothes if you're using the techniques at bedtime, which are perfect so long as they're warm enough, but don't forget that your own clothes should be comfortable too.

Your posture helps to support and encourage the experience you want to create for your child, so aim to sit in a way that reflects an alert but relaxed and comfortable state of mind. You can read the stories or do the meditations snuggled up cosily in bed, or sat on a chair or on the floor. But your child might enjoy them most lying down. See what works best for both of you.

Your child can keep their eyes open or closed – whatever feels more comfortable. If they feel drowsy, it can help to keep the eyes open softly to let in more stimulation. Alternatively, if you want to encourage sleep, closing the eyes can take them into a gentle, restorative sleep. We sort out many of life's difficulties in our dreams.

Now turn the page to find three relaxing guided meditations to help develop an increased sense of calm and awareness in your child's everyday life.

Golden Light Mindful Breathing

Mindfulness meditations help children to develop more focus and self-awareness. This exercise introduces your child to the experience of paying attention to the breath, linking it with the powerful visual image of flowing, golden light. It's a simple, quick practice that, once they've tried it out a few times, can be helpful in everyday life – if they are upset and need to calm themselves down, for example; or if they need to settle their mind and focus for a particular task. Before you start, ask your child to get into a comfortable, cosy position. Then, gently read the following words out loud to them:

"Notice how you are feeling.
Take a long, slow, deep breath in through your nose.
And then a long, slow breath out through your mouth.
Take another long, gentle breath in
and feel your body fill with air;
then breathe a slow breath out.
Let your body soften and feel nice and cosy.

Now, imagine that your breath is a beautiful, soft, golden light.
Make your next breaths long and gentle,
first in, then out.
Imagine your body is filling with soft, golden light
with each new golden breath

from right up at the top of your head,
flowing down, down,
out along your arms to your hands,
gentle, golden light flowing to the tips of your fingers.
As you continue to breathe,
imagine yourself feeling cosier and cosier.

Feel the golden light flow down your back,
fill and relax your chest,
and then fill and soften your tummy,
before moving down into your legs,
into your feet,
then filling each of your toes.

As the golden light flows through you,
you feel more and more relaxed.
If you get distracted,
just notice your body again,
notice your breath
and imagine the golden light
filling you with warmth and ease.

Finally, as you breathe out,
let the golden light flow out of your mouth
into the air around you.

Notice how you are feeling now.
Well done!"

Cultivating Kind, Friendly Wishes

By really paying attention to feeling, children can learn that, rather than emotions being fixed entities, they can change according to what we decide to do with them. The meditation below focuses on feelings of friendliness and appreciation, teaching your child how to be more compassionate toward others – and also toward themselves. Before you start, ask your child to get into a comfortable, cosy position. Then, gently read the following words out loud to them:

"Notice how you are feeling.
Take a long, slow, deep breath in through your nose.
And then a long, slow breath out through your mouth.
Take another long, gentle breath in
and feel your body fill with air;
then breathe a slow breath out.
Let your body soften and feel nice and cosy.

Now think of someone you like spending time with,
someone who makes you happy.
Maybe it's a friend or someone from your family.

Imagine that that person is with you right now.
Notice how you feel when you think of this person.
Whatever you feel is OK.

Now, imagine that you are looking at them
and telling them what you like about them.
It could be anything at all:
it might be their generosity
or the fact that they are your friend.

Next, imagine saying to them
that you wish them happiness,
you want them to be strong and healthy,
you want them to have lots of kind friends
and a peaceful life.

Imagine, as you are wishing your friend well,
that a beautiful flower is blossoming near his or her heart.
The flower can be any colour you wish.
As you think of your friend,
imagine that the fragrance of the flower
perfumes the air around both of you.

Now, imagine that your friend is looking at you
and saying all these things to you:
'I want you to be happy,
I want you to be healthy and strong,
I want you to feel peaceful.'

Notice how you are feeling now.
Well done!"

123

Visiting the Magical, Relaxing Garden

This meditation is inspired by the royal gardens in the story called "The Princess and the Precious Pearls" on pages 82–7. You can use it at any time to help your child become more relaxed and calm, and to give them more confidence to work out problems that may arise in their life. Before you start, ask your child to get into a comfortable, cosy position. Then, gently read the following words out loud to them:

"Notice how you are feeling.
Take a long, slow, deep breath in through your nose.
And then a long, slow breath out through your mouth.
Take another long, gentle breath in
and feel your body fill with air;
then breathe a slow breath out.
Let your body soften and feel nice and cosy.

Imagine yourself standing before two glittering golden gates
set into majestic stone walls.
Feel the ground below your feet as you look up at the gates.
Above you the sky is blue and the sun is shining.
You feel the warmth of the sun's kiss on your skin.

You reach out and touch the gates.
They swing open smoothly. The gates will open only for you.

This is your garden, yours alone.
You walk through the gates and onto a path.
The path glistens in the sunlight. You feel warm and safe.
You can smell the perfume of the many flowers in the garden.
You hear birds singing and chatting in the trees.
You hear the sound of water
as it tumbles into the fresh pools ahead of you.
Little silver fish dance through the water.

You sit on the edge of a pool and slip your feet
and legs into the water.
It feels cool and refreshing as it flows between your toes.
You feel completely at peace.
Feel the gentle movements of your breath, in through your nose
and gently, calmly, out through your mouth.
You straighten your legs to raise your feet above the water.
Water drops sparkle on your skin like millions of jewels.

You stand up and make your way back up the path.
You feel completely at peace.
As you reach the gates, you turn and look back at the garden.
You step through the gates and they close softly behind you.

Now, bring your attention back to your breathing.
When you feel ready, open your eyes.

Notice how you are feeling now.
Well done!"

125

Index of Values and Issues

These two complementary indexes cover the specific topics that the eighteen stories of this book are designed to address directly or by implication. The same topics are covered from two different perspectives: positive (Values) and negative (Issues). Each index reference consists of an abbreviated story title, followed by the page number on which the story begins.

Note from the Author

If anything in this book is inaccurate or misleading, I ask forgiveness of my teachers and of the readers for having unwittingly impeded their way. As for what is accurate, I hope that the reader can use it, so that they attain the truth to which it points.

Acknowledgements

Thanks to my friend Vimalacitta, for helping when I got stuck, and to the Watkins publishing team, for being a joy to work with. And of course to my wee dog Archie!